GW00750484

STRANDED ON DEATH ROW

DANNY BOY STEWARD

Trumbull Publishing Group

Atlanta, Georgia

Published in the United States by Trumbull Publishing
Group, a trademark of Trumbull Publishing, LLC.

Cover Design: Tara Mixon

Makeup: Burniemua@gmail.com

Photos: Merrill Robinson Jr.

To my mother, Dorothy J. Steward, and to my father, Robert

"Blood" Williams. Thank you so much for life and everything

you put in me... I promise to make you proud.

Dorothy J Steward 4/28/43- 2/8/95
Robert / Williams 12/25/43 - 2/8/11

Also to my kids, Ashlee, DJ, and Damarion, this is for y'all.

Contents

A note from Ginuwine

[Danny Boy] is one of few friends I have that absolutely kept it real with me at all times—even gave me money when I didn't have any, so I could eat. My brother, I'm proud of you and love you dearly. You came a long way, and your journey isn't over. [This is] such a great read, lil bro. Congrats. Handcuffs off.

Introduction

My life has been shaped by many ups and downs. Over the years, I have lost more family members and friends than I can even count. In so many ways, I have been at death's door. But very often, even in the midst of my sadness, I've been given the opportunity to experience things that many could only imagine. I have performed and collaborated with musical giants; I have shared my gift of song on stages all around the world.

I was only fifteen when I was signed to Death Row Records. As a kid, I was given a front row seat to the rise and fall of one of the most iconic labels in music history. For the most part, I grew up on Death Row—spending many of my formative years in the company of Suge Knight, and the late Tupac Shakur.

In the years following Tupac's death, and the subsequent demise of Death Row, there have been cinematic interpretations, articles, and books published about the label and its artists. But none could accurately tell the story, my story. This is it; this is the story of Danny Boy Steward.

Chapter 1: Oh Danny Boy

I was born on Halloween; my father was born on Christmas. In time, the significance of those days would become more evident than any of us could imagine. No one could have predicted how much I would teeter between life and death. Nor could they envision the trajectory my life would take. On that October night, my mother had just one purpose; it was to deliver a healthy baby boy. When she went into labor at Bob Belton's annual Halloween party, it wasn't a first time occurrence. She had gone into labor with my brother Gary at that same event just one year prior. Unfortunately, Gary didn't survive. But I did. Little did I know, survival would become the theme of my life.

As my father drove my mother to Loyola Hospital, the only comfort she could find was in the lyrics to Jackie Wilson's "Oh Danny Boy." When my parents arrived at the hospital, they learned that my mother had suffered several strokes. While the doctors worked to save her life, my mother focused her attention on my survival. Despite the risks to her own well being, she was committed to bringing me into the world. I was the seventh child, her baby, her Danny Boy.

During the delivery, and months after, my mother's health declined. Before long, she suffered one of her most critical strokes. This stroke left her unable to communicate as she once had—resulting in a lasting speech impediment. Music and poetry had been a large part of my mother's life. To no longer have access to her gift must have been difficult, but she lived without regret. Despite her limitations, she was happy to have given birth to me. I was her primary focus. Perhaps she knew that one day I would touch many lives.

Though the normal ear could not understand my mother, I could. Unless she was cursing someone out, there was no way to decipher her utterances. This new mother tongue was something only I could interpret. My other siblings had known her before, when she could speak clearly. But I only knew this voice—the one that limited her connection with the outside world. In a way, I guess it was a blessing. When I was old enough, I became her translator. In most families, children mimic the sounds of their parents, but even with her speech impediment, my mother taught me to speak correctly. She was even my first singing coach. She taught me the notes, and how to hold them. In this way, she was able to pass her gift on to me.

Speaking for my mother was not an easy task, but I did it. I would speak for her at the Public Aid Office, the Social Security Office; I even had to do it at my school. But that was the hardest of them all; the kids in elementary school were so cruel. They would sometimes tease me about the way she spoke. This would only add to the long list of things the kids at school teased me about.

I was more into music than anything else. That fact didn't sit well with the playground bullies, and some of the people I grew up with. In those days, if you were a boy and you didn't like sports, they would say you were girly. What made the situation worse was that my name was "Danny Boy." It was so easy for the kids to make fun of me and call me "Danny Girl." I can't count the number of fights I got into for that very reason. I lost most of those fights too. There would always be more than one person trying to jump me, but they knew not to bother me when they were alone. They wanted to be my friend when they were by themselves. And that's when I got the upper hand. One-on-one, I could easily kick their asses.

Fighting got me into trouble, but that wasn't the only thing. The days that I did attend school, I took my smart mouth with me. At least once a week, I would give the teachers hell. Most of the classes I chose to attend were simply platforms for me to be the class clown. I could've held onto that role, but God had other plans for me. It was his time to show up and show out.

Chapter 2: Music is My Dream

In Elementary School, my teacher noticed me singing in class. She suggested that I audition for the Soul Children of Chicago Choir. This was no small thing. The Soul Children was a largely known choir that was led by Walt Whitman.

When I went to the audition, I sang "Wind Beneath My Wings." That song got me a spot in the choir, but I soon realized that it wasn't the right fit for me. It was different from church, where I was known as the little guy who could sing. Here, I wasn't the only kid with a set of pipes. In the Soul Children, there were many talented singers; there were a lot of Danny Boys. I wanted more. I was desperate to find myself as a solo artist. After just two rehearsals, I was done.

There have been many instances that have shaped my musical life. I can remember one day in particular. My mother and grandmother attended one of my aunt Delores' concerts. It was something she did every year. This time, when they returned home, they were going on and on about one of the performers. "Ooh, that child know she sang that song," my grandmother said. I listened intently, wondering what child she was talking about. Her name was Deleon. I didn't know what Deleon Richards had done in her rendition of "If Anybody Asks You," but I knew that I wanted to garner the same type of reaction when I sang.

There was always singing when my family got together. Being the only child in the mix, I was like a sponge. As I listened to them sing old-school church songs, I paid attention to every nuance. After I learned the songs, I would join in—quickly catching my note. My uncles and aunts would tell me stories about how their neighbors would wait out on the porch just to hear them rehearse. That excited me, and kept me dreaming of my own time in the spotlight.

Soon I started singing at our church more often. Most Sunday's, I'd be at Greater Jerusalem Baptist Church— singing my face off. It was most certainly to the delight of my mother. It was like she was experiencing her gift through me, molding me into the singer that she knew I would be. She was constantly teaching me new songs to help me further develop my voice. She would be pointing to the floor for me to bring my note down, or pointing to the ceiling for me to bring my note higher. She would smile as she coached me, and cry whenever I sang. It was quite an experience. She gave me her all, and I gave her my best.

While my mother coached, my grandmother quickly took on the role of booking agent. She put me on all of the programs at our church and she got me on programs at churches all over the West Side of Chicago. It was a familiar role for her; her kids were singers. My grandmother did the exact thing for me that people later in my life would get paid the big bucks to do. But it was different for her. She did it out love. And while she didn't understand the business aspect, she fully grasped the Psalmist part. I would sing on the front porch, on top of garbage cans, at the houses of friends and neighbors—everywhere I could.

My aunt Delores sang lead vocals on The Thompson Community Choir's, "It's Gonna Rain"—a popular standard in gospel world, and especially in Chicago. When she and I sang on the same program, she decided to take me under her wing. She taught me a lot about stage presence. In fact, I learned something new every time I saw and heard her sing. Because of Aunt Delores, I was not afraid to sing in front of large crowds. I watched her sing all over the city. Sometimes she would get me on the program with her. And as I matured, she began to let me take on the bookings she couldn't make.

My aunt Joanne booked even more venues for me. In addition to booking, she became my first unofficial stage manager. She would say to me, "Don't sing too much; make them want more." And I would watch her as I sang. She would give me a look that let me know that I had given enough. It was great to have that level of support at such a young age. And it was a blessing to be part of a musical family. They always knew of some church, or event I could sing for. That level of encouragement and support contributed greatly to my success. By the time I was a teenager, I had performed at over 200 events. Whether it was a funeral, a wedding, church, or park districts; you name it, I probably performed there.

When I was thirteen, my mother had a heart attack. Following this heart attack, she had her first open heart surgery, which gave me even more responsibility. I remember those days like yesterday. The doctor had taken a vein from her leg to run through her heart valve, which left her two incisions, one under her breast and another on her leg. I was responsible for cleaning the incisions and changing the gauze. It was painful for her; she would cry all night long. And she would call out, "Jesus, help me" and "Oh Lord, oh Lord, Oh Lord." There was nothing I could do to ease the pain, and that was difficult to accept. But as time went on, my mother began to get a little better, and her incisions began to heal.

I worried about my mother day and night. It was this constant uneasiness that led me to my first encounter with God. I mean, God for myself. It wasn't my grandmother praying on my behalf, or someone else covering me. It was me who got on my knees and petitioned before him. As I listened to my mother crying in the next room, I did the only thing I could do. I prayed as I cried along with my mother; I asked God to heal her.

By graduation my mother was barely walking, but she made it. I sang "It's So Hard to Say Goodbye." When I walked across the stage, my mother cried like I had graduated from college. She loved me without question; I was a Mama's boy. When I was wrong, I was right in her eyes. My uncle William and my uncle Henry couldn't stand that. They thought that she should have whopped my ass for everything I did. When she didn't, my uncle Henry would jump on me, and punch me in the nose. Sometimes he would just kick my ass for no reason at all. When his sons and I fought, he would break us up and beat me himself. Sometimes I got my ass kicked by him, other times by his sons. Occasionally, I got my ass kicked by all of them.

My mother was always back and forth between my father's and my grandmother's homes. As she got sicker, she spent more time with my grandmother, but my dad was always there for her. After getting my ass kicked one time too many, I got sick of that shit and decided that I would move in with my father for a while. He was renting a room from a woman named Mrs. Williams. She was a friend of my father's and she had known me since I was a little boy. She was nice and treated me like I was her own, so I started calling her grandma.

Grandma Williams and my father lived on the second floor of a building on North Drake Street. I lived downstairs with Grandma William's daughter, Marilyn. She easily became my adopted aunt. I called her Tee-Tee. She loved me like I was her blood nephew. Her kids, Iesha, G-No, and Tony were like my cousins.

One thing about Grandma Williams's house was there was always a party going on. Her and my father would drink and play the blues all night long. During those times, Grandma would call me in front of her and say to me, "Sing something for Grandma." Before I could even begin to sing, she would say, "What Grandma say?" That was my cue, and if I didn't do what she said, Grandma would cuss me out!

I would sing church songs and other songs I had learned from records they played. I loved singing so much that I used to have concerts on the front porch so all of my neighbors could hear me sing. If they weren't at home, I would find cans, line them up, and sing to them. My taste in music was quickly expanding. In this new environment, I had become a fan of what people in the church called "secular music." But this didn't stop my mother and grandmother from encouraging me to sing the music I loved.

There were other perks to living with my father. I was able to hang out more with my older cousin, Boo, who was also known as Wild Style of the Hip-Hop recording artists, Crucial Conflict. He was also an adopted nephew of the Williams family. Wild's family lived on the block behind us. He was the driving force behind Crucial Conflict. At that time, Crucial Conflict consisted of Wild Style, Kilo, Tony and G-No. I would watch them intently as they rehearsed songs and choreography for shows. That's when I really learned how to sing outside of the church.

Wild would have me singing at Orr talent shows, block parties, clubs, and any other place they were performing. At times, I would be the only singer in the show. Orr's talent shows were off the chain. They would host artists like Twista, Do or Die, and R. Kelly. At least one of these acts would perform in each talent show, if not all of them.

During these times, my mother suffered another heart attack, which led to her triple bypass. I moved back home, and transferred from Orr to Crane High School. Transferring to another school didn't bother me because I was ready to leave the school choir. They weren't the best, and with my short attention span, I felt that I had given them long enough to get their stuff together. Many people went to school for an education, but I was there for the melodies.

Chapter 3: Definition of a Player

As soon as I arrived at Crane High School, I joined the chorus. It didn't take long for me to gain some popularity. I was a singer, and the other kids responded well to my voice. Soon after I transferred, I met up with Jesse, Willie, and Greg. They sang too, so it wasn't long before we decided to form a group. We called ourselves "Definition of a Player," DOAP for short. We hung out every day—singing, writing, and performing at Crane and Park Districts.

In order to perform, we needed to have outfits. As high school students, our funds were basically non-existent. We knew that we would have to get jobs if we wanted to present ourselves as a real group. Collectively, we decided that we would work at McDonalds. God was with us because we didn't even have to fill out an application. We wrote a jingle and sang it for the owner, Mrs. Milton. After we sang, all we had to do was give her our Social Security numbers. The next day she had uniforms ready for us. She was an incredibly understanding boss. I mean, there were times when we would go missing for days. Very often, we would take off without notice, and she would let us come back to work. I don't think any other boss would allow that kind of inconsistency. But she would have us there, working and singing on the front line.

We entered talent shows throughout the city, and we won most of them by performing songs by the groups we looked up to. We sang songs from Boyz II Men, Jodeci, and H-Town. We thought we were like the baby version of Jodeci with a Boyz II Men style of harmony. I could sing "Knocking the Boots" just like Dino from H-Town. After some time, Jesse and I moved in with my sister, Celestine, whom we affectionately called, Peaches. Peaches always supported me. She would always be the person sitting in the front row making the most noise. It was only natural that she became the manager of DOAP. Even though she had her own children, and was living in the projects, she found a way to feed us and make sure that we were taken care of. Living with Peaches was a good move for me. She believed in my talent, and did what was necessary to make sure I focused on honing my craft. She took on a leadership role, and quickly recruited partners. Booby, Ronald and Lisa became her co-managers.

Once our team was formed, we had more time to focus on our craft. We didn't have to worry about what we were going to wear, because Lisa and Peaches chose our outfits, and Booby and Ronald paid for them. They all got together and took the music game seriously. They even created a company called Synergy. But the formation of the company brought about a host of new rules. The one that bugged me the most was "No outside singing." That shit got on my nerves because I wanted to sing wherever I was. Before these new rules came into play, people could ride anywhere near our school and find us singing, but this changed it all.

It wasn't long before I lost interest in DOAP. We had been doing the same shows weekend after weekend, and wore the same outfits show after show. We *always* wore blue shorts and a white shirt with a blue stripe. I wanted a change; I needed a change. I figured Ronald and Booby felt the same as I did. Somehow I always seemed to know when it was time to move to the next level.

I talked to my group members about what I felt, but to my surprise, they were comfortable with the status quo. They told me that I should just chill out and stop trying to be the leader. The truth was, I was sick of the monotony; I had outgrown the group. I was at a point where I made it my goal to do everything possible to try and make it in the music business. To Peaches' and the team's displeasure, I left the group and moved out of the house. It was time for me to break away and go solo.

Chapter 4: Secular Music

My departure was probably the most difficult for Peaches. Out of everyone, she had been the most dedicated. She had taken on a motherly role, and was extremely concerned about my education, and my safety. Those were things she felt she could control as long as I was under her roof. And while her concerns were valid, I was determined to create something on my own. More than anything, it was a spiritual move for me. Throughout my life, I'd always had the spirit of discernment. I could see and feel things before they happened. So I followed that intuition.

I quickly searched out other avenues for creative expression. I started going back and forth to the studio watching Wild Style produce songs for Crucial Conflict. Wild Style was someone I looked up to. As an artist, he was the complete package. He had the looks, and he was rhythmically astute. He believed in my talent. In fact, it was him that pushed me to try singing R&B. I was known for singing church songs; now I was trying my hand at soul music.

While Wild Style and the other artists were recording, my cousin Tony was trying to get me into the booth. Before long, he helped me do just that. I went into the studio and recorded "If It takes All Night" with one of Crucial Conflict's producers, Dwayne Drain, whom we called, Uncle Foo. I sang: *I think it's about time you stop resisting, and give it all you've been missing. Tell me what I gotta do...* It was the best feeling! I was finally working on my own music, recording my first single, and going to school whenever I felt like it.

Shortly after recording that first single, Crucial Conflict left Uncle Foo's label and began working with Shorty Capone and Lay-Mar Productions. They eventually formed the "Raw Dope" label. Wild Style, Kilo, Cold Hard, and Never began recording with Shorty. One day, Wild took me up to the studio to sing for Shorty. From there, I became Lay-Mar's first male R&B recording artist. Shorty Capone hooked me up with his producers. Reggie Lamb, Chuck and Mark and I were recording every day. Reggie Lamb was our writer and vocal producer. Nobody could put melodies together like that man. When I was in the booth, Reggie would be right there with me. He'd have his headphones on showing me the way the song was supposed to go.

As time passed, the label grew to include Crucial Conflict, Fu-Skee and myself. We began doing interviews with the local newspapers, and we were performing on all the local TV shows. Our music was also being played by Rick Party on WGCI, one of Chicago's largest radio stations. Rick Party really believed in me, and always showed a lot of love for my music. I was so encouraged by the label's success that I decided not to go back home. I was at the studio every day; I figured I might as well live there. And that's just what I did. I made myself a pallet on the floor—right underneath a 48-track SSL board.

The studio was in a sort of, commercial house. I had access to the kitchen and bathroom, but it would be a while before I'd get my own room. The time I spent sleeping under the control board signaled the birth of my music career. Living in the studio was like a musical womb. Eventually, I would move into a proper room with a bed, but that time was invaluable.

Shorty took care of me. He would feed me every day, buy me clothes, and try to get me to go to school. Despite his efforts, school was the last thing on my mind. I thought school was cool for someone who wanted to be a doctor or something, but I had other plans. My parents were completely unaware. The production company had assured them that I would attend school, and they trusted that I was.

While in the studio, this girl named Tameka came in to do some background vocals. I could tell she liked me, but she never said anything. One day we were sitting alone in my room in the back of the studio having conversation, and the next thing I knew, we were kissing. We kissed until my lips were swollen. Ugh. I didn't like that. After that day, I didn't want to kiss, or do anything else with her. She was much too aggressive. Plus, she had a friend who I was much more interested in. She had a badass body, a pretty face, and wore this red lipstick that captivated me. I'll never forget the day Tameka introduced us. I can still hear her say, "Danny, this is Trina. Trina, this is my friend Danny."

When Tameka left the room, all I could do was stare at Trina's *red* lips. I stared at those lips until I finally worked up the nerve to talk. "Damn, let me taste them lips," I said to her. She just looked at me like I was crazy, but I was hooked. Trina was older, much older than I was. I had just turned fifteen. She was a woman, and I wanted her. So I lied about my age. As cliché as it sounds, age was just a number to me. I didn't look fifteen, and I didn't carry myself like a kid either. I had grown up around older people, and had experienced much more than people twice my age. Trina was light-skinned with long hair. She had pretty bowed legs, a flat stomach, and a smell that was mesmerizing. I wasn't about to let my age be a hindrance.

Later that night, while Tameka was in the booth laying background vocals, Trina and I sat alone, flirting with each other. Before I knew it, I was kissing her. From that day on, Trina would come to the studio at least three or four times a week. After a couple of weeks, she came and spent the night with me. I was a kissing something back then. I wasn't very experienced when it came to sex; I had only been with one other girl. That night, we touched, kissed, and had the best sex. It made me feel like a grown man. It was the best thing next to singing, and by far the best studio session to date.

After that night, I wanted her to come to the studio every day to see me; I even changed my schedule. All I did was the studio…and Trina. Nothing else in my world mattered. Being with Trina was the first time I wanted something more than just music. After many months of daily visits, I never wanted her to go home. Before long, Trina moved in with me. Both of us were living in the studio. When we were strapped for cash, we would share an Italian Beef. They came in either a six, or a twelve inch, neither of which was enough for two hungry people.

After putting our time in at the studio, Shorty hired Pit Bull to shop for deals. With the right amount of money, and Pit Bull on the job, artists were almost guaranteed an in. By the time the demo was done, Pit Bull had it on everybody's desk. That meant that it was time to go out to LA and do the damn thing.

The only problem was, I had never flown before. All I could think about were the stories I'd heard about planes being shot out of the sky. I couldn't even process how a plane actually stayed in the air; I had always traveled by bus. The airplane was new, and frightening—much different than the Greyhound trips I would take with my mother. I was scared as hell, but excitement and anticipation quickly took

over. I was on my way to LA; I was fulfilling my dream.

Chapter 5: Welcome to Death Row

When we landed at LAX, it was early in the morning. The sun was shining and it was hot as hell. I was happy though. Everywhere I looked, I saw pretty women driving drop top convertibles. Of course there were other beautiful things like palm trees and landscapes, but at fifteen, my mind was open to adventure of a different kind. The scenery made me feel like I was in a movie; it was perfect. The only thing missing was my girl.

Just before I left for LA, the record label released promotional photos that listed my real age. When Trina found out that I was only fifteen, she went ballistic and cut off all communication with me. I was heartbroken, but the LA sunshine was just the cure I needed.

The following day, Pit Bull had meetings set up with Capitol Records, Scotti Brothers and Warner Brothers Records. He had also set up a meeting with Black Tie Records. This was the label that was run by the legendary

R&B group, The Whispers. It was a great experience. I was in the studio with the same artists my father had listened to. They were there, in the flesh, singing and recording. When they came out of the booth, I had a chance to meet and sing for them. By the end of the week, they made us an offer. Things were moving fast, but there were more meetings with other labels, which included the possibility for more offers.

The day before we met with Interscope Records, there was an Earthquake. We had only been in LA for three days. As the youngest artist on the label, I shared a room with Pit Bull. He was like my big brother.

We had stayed up late watching the Gospel Awards. The next morning, I woke up to my bed shaking. Pit Bull woke up at the same time, and immediately jumped up to shield me with his body. I was scared. I had never experienced anything remotely like this in Chicago. I didn't even know about that kind of natural disaster. It was the scariest shit in the world. Pit Bull did his best to calm me.

With his Bohemian accent, he told me, "It's going to be okay."

When the rumbling stopped, I noticed that the television screen looked like a rainbow had crashed into it. I heard a zap just before the hotel went pitch black.

Shorty Capone came banging on the door asking if we were safe. He came in with one of those fat pagers, the ones with a flashlight on it.

In the halls, there was chaos. The locals were running to rooms, and banging on the doors hysterically; while us out-of-towners were in a panic. The stairwell was so dark that we had to use the pagers to light our paths; it was scary. There were twenty floors between us and solid ground, and that building was swaying from side to side like a hip-hop church choir.

We reached the bottom of the stairwell after what seemed like forever. In the lobby, the chaos continued. A couple of miles down, a freeway had collapsed and killed an officer. People were anxiously trying to book flights out of there, but they'd have to wait. Not even the airport was immune to the effects of the quake.

Once the flights were back on schedule, two of the artists who had come with us left, and vowed to never come back to California again. We had started our LA adventure with Shorty Capone, Kilo, Reggie Lamb, Chuck, Mark, Doug, and Pit Bull. With Mark and Chuck on their way back to Chi, our crew was down to five. It was all or nothing for me. Despite my fear, I was staying. But there was a large crack down the side of the building, so we had to find another place to crash.

Once we found another hotel, I took a walk around the area to have a look at the damage. It was catastrophic, to say the least. But within a couple of days, people were beginning to try to return to their normal routines. For us, it was time to get back to business. Shorty had a contract on the table with Interscope Records.

When we entered the building on Wilshire Boulevard, we were met with security, and taken to the twelfth floor where we were greeted by a larger than life, Death Row Records logo.

While we were waiting for the Interscope execs, Suge Knight and the First Lady of Death Row (at the time), Jewell walked in. We followed them into the conference room, and once we settled, Suge said to me, "Bust something." I guess he thought I was a rapper. I quickly obliged, and belted out the lyrics from my original song "Drive By." Suge stopped me mid-performance. "Wait a minute. I want someone else to hear this," he said. He walked out, and when he returned, he had two white dudes with him. I would come to know them as Steve Berman and Jimmy Iovine—the owners of Interscope. Of course, at that time, I had no idea who I was singing for.

When Suge came back with them, he said to me, "Sing that song homie." So I sang it again. Suge was like, "Oh yeah Shorty, he tight." He was ready to do business.

Shorty went for the big bucks, "$350K" he said, but Suge was the better businessman; he countered with $275K. Man, we were celebrating before we even had a check in our hands. Death Row was like the Motown of the 90s, and I was happy to be there. With the deal on the table, we checked into the Mondrian.

The Mondrian Hotel was a luxury hotel where all of Hollywood hitters stayed when they were in town. We stayed in LA for about three weeks before we flew back to Chicago.

Trina still wasn't taking my calls, but I was pleading with her to give me a chance. After I had been home for about two weeks, Suge called Shorty and told him to get me back out to LA to start recording. The next day, Shorty flew me back into LAX.

This time, I wasn't afraid. I had already flown there and back, and survived an earthquake. Once I had gathered my luggage, I noticed a lady standing before me. She was holding a sign with my name written above the Jackson Limousine logo. When I got to the car, the driver grabbed my bags; it was all so surreal. They were treating me like a big time celebrity.

While riding in the limousine, I opened the window to make sure everyone could see me. The only limousine I had ever ridden in was for my Aunt Edna and Uncle Sonny's funerals. Now, I was riding in a luxury limousine, and it was just for me.

When we arrived at the hotel, I damn near fell out of my seat. "Hello Sir. Welcome to the Beverly Hills Peninsula Hotel," the bellman said as he opened my door. They were treating me like a VIP. There was even a key waiting for me at the desk—a key for fifteen year-old me? I ran fast as shit to my room and closed the door. The rate listed on the back of the door was $525 per night. What the hell? I had to look twice. I was tripping, because I was just a teenage boy from the West Side of Chicago. Now I was staying where the stars stayed. And when I discovered that I could order anything I wanted and charge it to the room, it was on! All I had to do was sign the paper. It was Jewell that showed me how to do this, but that wasn't all she taught me.

She and her friends would come up to my room early in the day, and staying the entire night. They would be ordering drinks, food, getting massages, and manicures right in the room. It really didn't matter to me. It was like one big ass party for about two weeks. We were living it up! Not one dime had to come out of my pocket. I was living the life.

Jewell would bring a new group of women every day. Shit, we were ordering Cristal by the dozens. At one point, everybody in the room had their own bottle; I never paid attention to how much any of it cost.

On one of the days, Jewell came to my room alone. We ate, drank champagne, and got toasted. Jewell was bold, and if she wanted something or felt some kind of way, she would say whatever she felt.

There I was, at the head of the bed, and she was sitting at the foot. She slid her body across the bed so that she could be closer to me. She leaned in and said to me, "Who is this crazy girl you got sprung, lil' boy?" I looked her in her face, and I said to her, "I'm not that little. Trust me; I'm grown."

"Show me," she said with a seductive look.

At this time, I was just barely sixteen-years-old. She was at least ten years older than I was. I tried my best to beat around the bush because I was scared as hell. But that didn't stop her from wanting me to show her what the deal was. Before I could say the next word, she put her hand in my pants, pulled my dick out, and started doing things to me with her mouth. She was a beast, and I enjoyed every moment.

Jewell and I kicked it like that a few more times. I guess she was feeling a young brother because she started hooking me up with all kinds of stuff. In fact, she rented me my first car. When I ended up getting pulled over and going to jail for driving without a license, she was the one to bail me out. When I needed a way to communicate with my people, she got me a phone.

One day I had the limo driver take me into Compton to meet with a hook-up Jewell had arranged for me. Before we arrived at the destination, the limo phone rang. It was Suge's assistant, Roy. He asked the driver how soon he could have me back at the office because Suge wanted to meet with me. The driver told Roy that we were out in Compton, and that it would take at least forty-five minutes for us to get back to the hotel. "No, no, no! You've got to be kidding me!" Roy said. The next voice I could hear was Suge's, "You fucking idiot! Bring that motherfucker to my office, now!"

Hearing Suge that mad put some fear in me. After all, he was Suge Knight of Death Row. I was afraid to face him, so I disappeared. I left all of my stuff, bought my own plane ticket, and flew my ass back to Chicago.

Shorty knew that I was scared, but he pleaded with me to go back. He said to me, "Nigga, you know I ain't gone let nothing happen to you." Shorty was his own version of Suge as far as Chicago was concerned. This was all the convincing I needed. Me, Kilo, and Shorty flew back to LA. When we arrived, Kilo stayed in his room and Shorty and I headed to Suge's office.

We waited hours for Suge to arrive. When he finally walked in, he was all in my face with his finger pointed damn near up my nose. "Do I look like I just fell of a banana truck?" he said to me. On the inside, I was shaking like a leaf. Shorty only sat there, watching. "Look. I know you young, but I will fuck you up! You spent $65K in one month!" Suge shouted. "One thing that I don't like is a Hollywood motherfucker," he said. And that was it. After that

frightening experience, I never gave Suge any more trouble.

After being that close to death, I knew I'd better behave.

Chapter 6: Thunderstorm

After my incident with Suge, I humbled myself and checked into the Le Montrose Hotel in West Hollywood, which was hardly a downgrade. I had heard that the R&B group, Jodeci had stayed there and that had me excited. Back in my DOAP days, we would sing their songs and mimic their performances. We wanted to be just like them. Only months before, I had been in Chicago dreaming of fame. Now I was walking and living in the same place my childhood idols had lived; I didn't take that for granted.

My time at Le Montrose was exciting. I constantly found myself in the presence of greatness—legends in the making. In fact, it was during my residence there that I met the man who would become the Notorious B.I.G. That meeting ended up costing me quite a bit of money, though. I had gone up to the rooftop to smoke. I guess he must have followed the trail of smoke. When he found me, he asked, "Where you get that chronic?"

In person, Biggie was as large as his persona. So I gave him a smoke, and from that moment on, we were smoking buddies. We literally smoked all night.

When I met him, he was writing the verse to what would become one of his most iconic songs. He walked around in just his socks. To be honest, they were the dirtiest things I had ever seen in my life. At that time, he was just getting ready to come out. Like many of the other artists at Le Montrose, Biggie was working on new music. He walked around with this raggedy notepad. And he just kept repeating the lyrics, "*Cause I see some ladies tonight, that should be having my baby...baby.*" He said that line until all my smokes were gone. When I went back to my room, I felt stupid as hell. I had just spent three hundred and fifty dollars on that sack. The next night, he smoked me out again.

It was good to be back in Cali, but I was missing my girl. I was a young, lovesick kid, and Trina was barely taking my calls. It took quite a bit of convincing to get her to agree to the trip, but I guess she had some love for the kid after all. I wanted her there, so I took the chance, and asked the label to fly her out. Maybe it was a bit of naiveté, or just me testing my limits, but whatever it was, it worked. Before I knew it, Trina was on a flight to LA. Initially, it was supposed to be a three-week trip, but to my delight, she ended up staying there with me.

While we were staying at the Mondrian, we learned that some of the cast from the Wayans Brother's show, "In Living Color" were staying there, including Jamie Fox. I got to meet a lot of people, but Bebe Winans and Jamie Fox were two of my favorites. Jamie was staring on "In Living Color" at the time, and Bebe Winans was gospel royalty. As big as the city was, the Hollywood community was pretty close knit. People connected over like interests. Jamie and I had music in common, and that was enough. We would sing, and he'd play the piano. He was a humble brother; there were no super star antics—just vocals and keys. Jamie was a friend, and kind of like my first celebrity neighbor.

After a while, it was time to change hotels again. When I moved to the next hotel, I had a chance to kick it with some of my future label mates. I met Chicago R&B group, B-Reazill, Snoop Dogg and Tha Dogg Pound, Nate Dogg, and some more of Suge's homies. At that time, Snoop was working on "Murder Was the Case." Snoop, Dre, Nate Dogg and Warren G were rehearsing for the Arsenio Hall Show. That's when Suge decided that I was going to come out during their set and do something. Suge said that he didn't care if I sang a church song or an oldie, it didn't matter. All he wanted to do was introduce me as a new artist: I wasn't even officially signed yet.

Suge always seemed to be one step ahead when it came to my career. It was no time before he brought DJ Quik on board. Quik was one of the most talented, gifted, artists I'd ever met. He and I clicked right away, and he quickly became my big brother and musical mentor.

Quik was more than a rapper. He was capable of producing across genre. He knew how to bring all the greatest musicians together, and that's just what he did when we recorded "Come When I Call." When we played the song for Suge, he went crazy. Even though the record was already being mixed, he insisted that it be placed on the "Murder Was the Case" album. That was a big moment for me. I started calling and telling people that I would be on the record.

I couldn't wait to get back to the hotel to tell Trina the good news. I had planned to take her out to a restaurant, but she wasn't feeling well. She had been nauseous and had started to vomit. Trina could be mean, but during this time, it had risen to another level. All of the symptoms pointed to pregnancy, so we took a trip to the nearest CVS and picked up a test. When we got back to the room, two little pink lines confirmed our suspicions; we were going to be parents.

The challenge of being a teenage parent was of little concern to me. I felt like an adult, and my career was on the rise. I felt that I was capable of caring for a child. I was excited and so was Trina. I quickly called my mom to tell her the news. For so long it had been my other siblings calling to tell her that she was going to be a grandmother; it was finally my time. My mother was over the moon. "When is she due?" she asked. I could tell that she was smiling from ear to ear, but when I asked her to give consent for me to marry Trina, she said, "You already married! I'm your wife." I'm certain that she would have made it happen if I pressed her, but the subject of marriage was short-lived. For the moment, we were focused on becoming parents.

Things were going good for me. I was working on my album and preparing to do Arsenio. I couldn't wait for my mother and grandmother to see me on television. It was hard for my grandmother to believe that I was actually working in LA because people had begun to spread rumors.

They told her that I was actually in LA selling drugs. When I would send my advances home to my mother and grandmother, it only fueled speculation. I didn't want my grandmother thinking that I was sending her drug money. Seeing me on television would finally put the rumors to bed. But we never made it to the Arsenio Hall Show. At the last minute, Snoop, Dre, and their crew decided to back out. They all came up with excuses, but whatever their reason, I secretly believed it was in response to Suge pulling Warren G. so that I could perform.

After the fiasco with the Arsenio Hall Show, I started to focus on the promotions for my record. There was a bit of a buzz as my name was popping up in magazines, and my image was on wrapped vehicles, and all over BET and MTV. I was so happy because I now had proof. When I sent home copies of my promotional album, I finally had something to show my grandmother to prove to her that I wasn't selling drugs. It wasn't the church music I had grown up singing, but I was singing nonetheless. Before this, I had been known as the church boy, but this was something totally different.

My mother was so proud that she took one of the albums to church. It was a big deal because she was on the Pastor's Aide Committee. To her defense, she had no idea about the lyrical content. She was just a proud mother sharing her son's accomplishments with her church family. I don't think that her, or my grandmother paid any attention to the lyrics. I mean, I was talking about sex, and quite explicitly. To my delight, they didn't harp on my marked departure from gospel. They were just happy to see me happy.

While things were good on the music front, they were beginning to fall apart on the home front. Trina and I had begun to argue. Trina was older, and more mature, but I thought she was being too motherly. I was hanging around guys who "handled" their women differently, so I began to bring that behavior home. I started feeling myself. I would call her out of her name—disrespecting her at every turn. Trina was right about a lot of things, but I couldn't get past her anger. In my mind, she was mean. In her mind, I had become someone other than the guy she had fallen for. Our relationship had gotten so bad that when we returned to Chicago for the holidays, I was in a limo to my grandmother's house, and Trina was in a Town Car on her way to her mother's.

When I arrived on 19th and Trumbull, there was a sea of people there to greet me. Everyone was out there; my childhood friends and I even some of my childhood bullies were in the crowd. People who had once made fun of me were out in the crowd trying to catch a glimpse; it was crazy.

The limo waited out front while I went into the house and took a nap on my grandmother's high bed. When I woke up, my grandmother had my Aunt Diane make me breakfast with my favorite, slab bacon—the thick cut that takes an hour to chew; it was good to be home.

When I finally went back outside, all my buddies were out there waiting for me on the porch. Those who could fit pilled into limo while the rest of the crew followed behind. We partied all night long, and into the next week. I gave to every person that asked. By the time I left, I had spent $15K partying, shopping, and just giving money away; it felt good. It was something my parents would have done. They were givers. If someone was in need, they would do what they could to help.

As much as my mother had sacrificed, I wanted to give something to her. That Christmas, I was able, for the first time, to give her a real gift. The only thing my mother wanted was a trench coat and a gold ring. I can't even describe the feeling I had. It was a small gesture, and it didn't cost much, but it felt good to make my mother smile.

Chapter 7: Done Deal

After the holidays, I was eager to get back to LA. It was finally time to sign my contract. The only problem was that my parents wanted me to wait and retain a lawyer. But that would take more time, and I was ready to make everything official. Suge and his lawyers had already been asking for the contract, so I ended up forging my mother's name. I was a kid from Chicago with a $275K deal on the table. There was no way I was going to risk waiting on a lawyer.

About a week after the contract was signed, the label gave Shorty a check for the total amount. This was standard business, as he was responsible for getting me to LA. He had hired Pit Bull, who had essentially got me the deal. So I expected that he would need to recoup expenses, plus a small percentage. But that wasn't how things went down. Suge's first wife, Sharitha, met us at Citizens bank. After Shorty cashed the check, he got into the car with

Sharitha and gave her $100K in cash. When we got back to the hotel, Shorty gave me $25K. And that was the last time I saw him. The same person who got me started on Death Row, had taken my money, and left me stranded.

It took me some time to realize that I had been scammed. I was a teenager, and $25K was still a lot of money. But when Shorty didn't return, I knew that I had been taken advantage of. It was difficult to process. As the artist, I received less than anyone involved. Shit. Suge wasn't even supposed to get paid out of that money. When Shorty took off with the advance, he also left me with the responsibility of taking care of the other guys that had come out with us. Fuskee and some of the members of Crucial Conflict were still in LA. That $25K wasn't going to last long. It was a hard hit, but I had to get back to work. Plus my label was depending on me, and I needed to deliver.

I went back in the studio with Quik and his production manager, G-One. During those sessions, I had a chance to meet with musicians that were playing for so many big names in Hollywood. G-One had connections with them all because he had just returned from Brandy's, "I Wanna Be Down" tour. Man, we were in that studio recording every day. Quik's samples were minimal because he mostly used live musicians. The music was incredible; it was organic. Those were some of my best sessions. I was high off the music alone. But like many times in my life, that high was short-lived.

When I got home, there was a message on the machine about my mother; she had fallen ill. I was anxious to see her, but my grandmother told me that she was all right, and that she just wanted to let me know she was back in the hospital. She told me to stay in LA and continue working. I couldn't agree until I actually heard my mother's voice. I quickly placed a call to The University of Chicago Hospital. When I called, my mom answered and we talked on the phone for a long time. She was just laughing in her soft voice. The laughs gave me hope that she would be okay.

Suge called to check on me. He asked what hospital she was in, and the next thing I knew, he had filled her hospital room with flowers. Within a week, my mom was released. She returned home to my grandmother who had just had surgery herself. Heart issues were common in my family, and it wasn't unusual for one or both of them to be sick. My mom would sit on the couch, and my grandmother would sit in her Lazy-Boy chair; they would take care of each other. Each time I called to check on my mother, she would ask if Trina had given birth yet. "Not yet," I'd tell her. I was excited to share the news that we were having a girl, and that I had been there for the ultrasound. But we would all have to wait to meet her. It would be another four months before our little princess would arrive.

Even though I had signed a record deal, and had a baby on the way, I was still a minor. Living apart from my parents created a legal problem. I needed a guardian who could be in the state of California with me. Because of her heart condition, my mother couldn't travel. My father was in his sixties, and too settled in Chicago to pick up and move to California. I considered Trina, but I wasn't going to set myself up like that. If I gave her that kind of control over me, I would really have to come in the house when she said so. *Oh hell no!* I wasn't having that.

When I went to Suge with my dilemma, he told me that he had talked to my mom in the hospital, and promised her that he would take care of me. Suge said to me, "Danny Boy, you always with me. I might as well adopt you—as long as you don't go all Hollywood on me." Once his lawyer drafted the documents, we had them signed, and I officially became a Knight.

Mid January, I was in the lobby of the hotel waiting for Dave Foreman who had been in on most of my sessions. I was sitting in the bar at the window when he arrived. When he came in, he had Darius McCray with him. Darius was one of the stars of the television show *Family Matters*; he played Eddie Winslow. Darius was accompanied by his cousin who was working on music with him. Like so many others in the industry, we connected over music. We exchanged numbers and vowed to keep in touch.

A few days later, Darius called me and told me that his cousin had died in his sleep. It was the same cousin that I had just met a couple of days earlier. Darius wanted to know if he could put me on the program. It was a familiar place for me. I was always singing at funerals. It was actually an honor to be asked. When I met Darius' mother and siblings, they were some of the nicest people. They treated me like they had known me for years, and quickly became my extended family.

The day of the funeral, I sang a solo, and Darius and I sung a duet. After the service, I had a chance to meet the rest of his family. They reminded me of my own family. They came together like we would when we experienced loss. They showed so much love and affection for one another. I could tell from their conversations that they saw each other all the time. It wasn't just funeral talk; they weren't in love with each other just because someone had died.

After the funeral, I got back to recording my album. I was working with some great producers, and things were looking good. "Murder Was the Case" had dropped, and could not be kept on the stores shelves. It was the shit! People all over were hearing my voice. My dreams were coming true.

I met MC Hammer and Keyshia Cole during this time. Hammer brought her up to Death Row. She was trying to be an artist. She would hang around the label and travel with us from time to time. We bounded like sibling; I was the big brother. I even gave her vocal lessons at one time. Those were the good times. Before long, she too would grow up and show her ass.

Chapter 8: Dear Mama

February 8, 1995

I had been in the studio working on the song "Call on Me" with Kevin Lewis (son of jazz pianist Ramsey Lewis). Studio sessions were normally easy for me, but that night, I kept getting hung up on one part. I just couldn't get it right. The part was so simple that the guys couldn't understand why I was having such difficulty. Something was off. Before I could give it much thought, Death Row's secretary came in with an urgent message. I rushed to the phone. On the other end was my grandmother. She told me that my mother had gone back into the hospital. "You need to come home," she said. In the past, my grandmother had always told me to stay. "You work," she would say. This time, she was calling on me to come home. She had confirmed what my spirit already knew. It was the reason I couldn't focus in the studio. My mother was on her deathbed.

I immediately called my homie, Young Buck. He was my first friend in LA. If there was anyone I could count on, it was him. When he got there, things went from bad to worse. There was a terrible storm, and a pending evacuation for the area. Just two blocks away, the streets had flooded, and the traffic lights were under water. Flights were delayed and I wouldn't be able to get out of LA until the next day. I couldn't sleep; I paced the floor all night—calling my grandmother periodically to pray. I was desperate to be by my mother's side. I could feel hear leaving.

That next afternoon, I called my grandmother to tell her I was on the way. When I dialed her house, my aunt Diane answered the phone. My aunt had suffered brain damage several years prior, and was subject to speak without restraint. So when I asked her to let me speak to my grandmother, she said, "Mama gone to the hospital, Dorothy died." She just spit it out like it was nothing. It was a brutal way to find out that my dear mother was gone. "You coming up here?" she said. I dropped the phone and ran out of the door. I didn't know what to do. I sat in the middle of the driveway in a puddle of water. Young Buck was trying to get me off the ground. Trina was calling for the other people in the house to help me. She even called Suge to see if he could help. When she finally got him on the phone, he kept telling me, "It's all right, it's all right." He offered to fly out with me, but I chose to go alone.

That five-hour flight to Chicago seemed like it took the whole day. When I finally landed, I rushed down the stairs to the arrival area and into the car of my regular driver. We took the normal route, but traded our normal banter for a solemn drive. My friends were waiting for me when we pulled up. Through tears and nods, I made my way upstairs to my grandmother's home. When I opened the door, there was a sea of faces looking out at me, and at the center, my grandmother sat in her Lazy Boy—my mother's chair absent her usual smiling face. It was real. She was gone. I put my head in grandmama's lap and cried until I fell asleep.

Early the next morning, we woke up and prepared to go to the funeral home to make the arrangements. When we arrived, the Funeral Director took me back to view my mother's body. My insides felt as if they had dropped to the floor. It's impossible to explain the feeling. We had been so deeply connected, now I was making plans to bury her. It was more than overwhelming; I was crushed, but there was so much to do.

February 12, 1995

When we arrived at the funeral home, there were cars lined up further than I could see. As I walked up the stairs, I recognized old classmates and teachers that I hadn't seen since my eighth grade graduation, people from the radio station, and many more people that I didn't know. People were coming in, one after another. I sat in disbelief as people walked up and offered their condolences.

The service began with the reading of my mother's favorite scripture, John 3:16. After the scripture, there was a solo. Jewell walked down the aisle and up to the podium. I hadn't been sure that she would make it, so it was a pleasant surprise. Everyone's eyes were fixed on her because her breasts were damn near spilling out of her shirt. Nonetheless, I was happy to have her there. She was the only artist that showed up to support me.

When it was time for me to sing, it was the most difficult performance of my life. I wasn't Danny Boy the artist; I was a child who had just lost his mother. When I walked past her casket, I almost fell out, but I had to pull it together. I felt a sense of responsibility to sing the way my mama had taught me. I sang the calm, meditative gospel standard, "When I See Jesus." Though I had sung it many times before, I could only make it to second verse; I cried throughout the rest of the song.

I buried my mother the next day. When I arrived at the funeral home, I was able to see my mama one final time. I just sat there looking at her body. It was painful, but I couldn't move. I sat there looking at my mama until the funeral directors came to cover her face up and close her casket. People had to hold me up as they lowered her body into the ground. I know it was God that brought me through; it had to be. If it weren't for God, I would have lost my mind.

A week later, I decided to do what my grandmother had always told me to do; I went back to work.

Chapter 9: Back on the Row

When our flight landed in LA, Trina went back to the apartment and I went to Suge's place. He and I sat and talked for a long time. I don't think Suge really knew exactly what to say, but he kept talking to me anyway. Every time he'd speak, it would take me back to my mother. I would just sit there and cry. Even he was fighting back tears.

The support he gave after I lost my mother helped to cement our relationship. That's when Suge really took me under his wing. We talked about Shorty's disappearance, and how he made off with $125K. Once Suge found that out, he really made sure he looked out for me. He began to treat me as if I were his real son. Some of the other label mates didn't like that, and it silently stirred up some animosity between them and I.

Later on that day, I went to Can-Am studios to finish the song that Kevin Lewis and I had been working on before I left. "I'll Be There" was a song about loving someone, but having to let them go. This time when I sang, my pain and passion were more evident than ever. Before I'd left, I was just a kid who hadn't experienced much. But now, I was becoming a man and a father in a world without my precious mother. I put all my emotion into that song.

After my mother's passing, I became more passionate about my craft; music was healing. I knew that my mother would have wanted me to sing as hard as I could. As I sung in the studio, I would have visions of my mother point to floor or ceiling to tell me to sing high or low. I had to do it.

*****

As the weeks passed, Trina's contractions began to become persistent, and the false alarms continued. On March 4th, it was finally the real thing. The contractions were coming closer together. At about 10 p.m., Trina's water broke. I anxiously paced the floor, nervous and not sure what to do. Once I finally put her in the car, we drove from The Valley to Cedar Sinai Hospital. It was the hospital that all the people with money went to. I thought I was balling. So I was taking Trina to the place the stars gave birth. But while we had money and other stuff, we didn't have insurance. And Cedar Sinai was quick to direct us to the nearest county hospital. We got back in the car and drove back to The Valley; all while, Trina was still in labor.

I called everyone I knew in LA to get help finding a hospital. One of my homies told me to go to a hospital in Sylmar. He assured us that we wouldn't have any problems there. By the time we got there, I had to go in to get someone to help us. When they came out and saw that she was in labor, they immediately rushed her into Labor and Delivery.

We sat all night waiting for her to have the baby. At the break of day, the contractions even were closer together, but not close enough for her to deliver. They decided to induce her labor.

While we were waiting for Trina's labor to progress, I got a call from my boy Darius telling me that he was downstairs. I told him the room number, and he came up immediately. Darius and I sat by the bed, counting the time in between the contractions. By the time the Mid-wife came in to tell us that it was time, Trina was hollering and screaming. The pain had gotten so bad that she actually kicked the mid-wife from one side of the room to the other.

When the mid-wife got off of the floor, she walked out and left Darius and I in the room with Trina. It was the craziest thing. Darius was on one side of the bed, and I was on the other. Trina was pushing, but she was having a hard time. It looked like we would have to deliver the baby ourselves. Darius was a trooper though. He and I were there coaching Trina through, "Come on, you got this," we kept saying to her. She was pushing for a while before we saw the crown of the baby's head. We yelled for the doctor to come in and help us; he made it just in time. Within ten minutes, the baby was born.

Just as the baby began to cry, I heard the doctor say, "Congratulations! It's a girl!" As soon as he said that, the tears began to roll down my face. I couldn't explain the joy I felt holding my first-born for the first time, nor could I explain the pain that I felt knowing that my mother was just one month shy of seeing my baby girl. We named our princess, Ashley Dotrinae Lashae Steward. It was a combination of mine and our mothers' names.

After aiding in Ashley's delivery, Darius said, "Man, I was here, so I earned the right to be the god-father." I didn't have a problem with that. He had definitely proven himself. Since he was friend enough to assist in the birth of my first child, he had more than earned the title. Plus, Darius was good people; it was a good choice.

Three day later, Darius called me at the studio and asked me to meet him at my spot. Man, I got to my house and Darius jumped out the car. His back seat was full of stuff for Ashley. When he popped the trunk, and that was full too!

"Come on man, and help me take this up." He said to me. "I gotta get back to the set." He was passionate about his godfather role, and this further confirmed that he was the right choice.

I was excited to bring my daughter home, but not so happy with our location. Before the baby was born, I had moved Trina from the hotel to an apartment. Our place was super nice, but it was in a horrible neighborhood, and I didn't feel safe living there. Suge had no idea we were living in Van Nuys. When he found out, he quickly found another place for us to live, but first I had to go check it out to see if I liked it.

Once again, I called my homie Young Buck and we went to check out the home. It was a beautiful, resort-like property. I didn't care how it looked on the inside; I was ready to move in that day! I called Suge and told him that I wanted to move in immediately.

Suge had the placed furnished, and a few days later, the office hired a nanny. Things were getting better by the day.

Chapter 10: East Coast vs. West Coast

Months had gone by, and DJ Quik and I alone had recorded at least 16 songs. We shot my first video for "So in Love," a remake of the Leroy Hudson joint. When they asked who I wanted my leading lady to be, I told them Tatiana Ali. There was no bigger actress than her at the time. I wanted to see how much power I had, and what do u know? I got Tatiana Ali, one of the stars of "Fresh Prince of Bel-Air." Tatiana was incredible. She was sweet, modest, and sexy as hell. We were around the same age, so I quickly seized the opportunity to flirt with her during the shoot.

Days after my video shoots with Tatiana Ali, Suge called and told me that we were going to the Source Awards. We were listening to oldies on a private jet when Suge said to me, "For every song you know, you can have this." He was waving a stack of hundred-dollar bills at me. It was something he did every time we rode in a car or plane, so I was ready. I had been at home practicing every oldie I could think of.

Suge didn't know that my dad had raised me and my siblings up in the Continental Lounge on 5th Avenue and Trip, in Chicago. My daddy always made sure I had quarters for the jukebox. By the time we arrived at the Ritz Carlton Hotel in NY, I had made about four thousand dollars playing Suge's game.

At the hotel, I checked into one of the flyest rooms they had. There were on-demand options years ahead of cable. Suge had the biggest suite in the hotel. His had four bedrooms and a huge great room. I mean it was huge! He ordered hundreds of dollars in food and let us order anything we wanted.

By that night, my god-brother Obie had come in town. We took a quick meeting, and headed to a local restaurant where we chilled with Suge, Russell Simmons, and some other big names. I ended up throwing up all over the table. It wasn't a great moment for me. They were heated, so Obie and I headed back to the hotel.

I was in my room relaxing and watching movies when I ended up falling asleep on the floor. I am from the West Side of Chicago. I was raised up sleeping on pallets on the floor at my grandmother's house. And now, blessed with the opportunity to sleep in a bed at one of the best hotels, I chose to fall asleep on the floor.

That next afternoon, when I went to Suge's room, the table was covered with food, and all of the seats at the table were occupied by women. Suge introduced me to the ladies and I went around the table hugging each and every one of them.

One of the women at the table was Mary J. Blige. The other women were the baby mama's of some other artists in the industry. There was one I recognized. She was Puffy's (the CEO of Bad Boy) baby mama, Misa. I ended up chilling with them most of that day. We drank, smoked, and had a good time.

At the end of the evening, all of the girls left except Misa; she stayed behind. It was funny how Suge was in the room with her for hours. Suge got a kick out of sleeping with other people's women. A large part of his war was sleeping with your girl. He would joke, "Puffy's bitch *in* my room." It was like a game to him. People toss around many theories about the origins of the East Coast, West Coast beef, but I know that a lot of it was about women.

I was in my room chilling with my bro when Suge called and asked me to come up to his room. "Come alone," he said. When Suge made calls like that, I never knew what to expect. I thought somebody was about to get their ass kicked. But when he opened the door, I could see Misa sitting at the foot of the bed with a sheet half-wrapped around her body. Mary J. was sitting on the couch. Suge said to me, "Mary wanted me to call you back up here. She came back to see you, but she didn't want her girls to know." So there I was, chilling with this superstar who had made a special effort to see me.

We were in the living room of Suge's suite talking and drinking. When room service knocked on the door, she fell to the floor like she was fighting in Iraq. I said to her, "You good? It's just room service at the door." I opened the door, and room service came in and set up our food and drinks.

I wondered what the fuck was wrong with her, but then I remembered that she had a man. And it had been rumored that he had physically abused her. I thought that might be the reason for her reaction, but it was still crazy to me. I had been with Death Row for a while, and I wasn't used to people being around us and scared; that just didn't happen. No one would get past Suge's people. She would be fine as long as she was with us.

After a while, we were laughing and telling jokes and just having a good time. It started getting late, so we went into my room inside of Suge's suite. She went to lay down on the bed; I sat in a chair. "Why you sitting over there?" she said to me. I was nervous as hell! I mean, I was a fan of hers. Trina was crazy about her and her music. And here I was, lying in the bed with her.

When she put my arms around her, the talking and laughing shit was all over. Before I knew it, she backed up against me. I was trying everything in my power for her not to feel how hard my dick was; that didn't work. She backed up into me every time I moved away. Before I knew it, we were kissing. I took her clothes off and kissed her neck. I tasted her body. It tasted better than I imagined. You haven't tasted anything until you've tasted Mary J. I got on top of her, and she wrapped her legs around me. I could tell by the moans and the screams that I was pleasing her. It didn't matter to me that I didn't have a condom on, because I wanted to make a baby with her and take it back to the hood. When we were done, we fell asleep, woke up, and did it again.

I wish I had had a camera phone back then. I think I would have been on some bullshit. I'm just kidding, but I have to say, I was charged up. After that encounter, I would never be able to listen to her music in Trina's presence.

I waited like a gentleman to make sure she was gone. But as soon as she left, I ran straight downstairs to my room where Obie was sleeping. I opened the door and jumped up and down on the bed like an eight year old kid.

When Obie woke up, and started wiping his eyes. I was like, "Nigga! Guess who I just hit?" I put my hand in his face so he could smell. He pushed my hand away, but when I said whose smell it was, he wanted to smell it again. All that was on my mind was how I wished I could call and tell everybody I knew.

When she left, I thought it was just going to be a one-night thing, but she left her number on the nightstand. At least I had a chance, I thought.

She had my young ass flying back to NY over and over again. Now that I'm grown, I wish I could do it one more time.

Later that day, Suge took us to the mall so we could get ready for the Source Awards. We were tearing the mall down. At this time, Death Row was into it hard with Bad Boy. Every artist that was involved with Death Row was there. With Snoop on the ticket to perform, Suge had two rows reserved for his artist and all of our people. When we arrived to the arena where the awards were being held, we mobbed in about one hundred deep.

When the time came for Death Row to receive the award, Suge told me to come up. I felt like I was outside of my body! I was loose as hell as I walked up to the steps. Before shaking things up, Suge got on the mic and gave his thanks and shit. After that, he made that infamous statement, "Any artist that wanna be an artist and wanna stay a star, and don't wanna have to have to worry about the Executive

Producer being all in the videos, all on the record, dancing…come to Death Row." He ended that statement like the boss he was.

All the Death Row artists started clapping, laughing and standing up. I was yelling, "Westside" while Suge was talking. I was throwing up Mob on one hand and Four on the other hand. The audience was booing us like a motherfucker. When Snoop and Dre came on stage, Snoop was yelling, "The East Coast ain't got no love for Snoop and Dre?" He said that shit with so much aggression, but we were in NY. They were going to stand by the East Coast. People in the crowd just kept booing, but the show went on.

When Faith and Puffy got on stage, Puffy was on his game. He knew how to make himself look good in the media. He congratulated Snoop, Dre, and Death Row and said that the East Coast West Coast thing needed to stop.

Later that night, Suge and Puffy ran into each other at the club. Like always, Suge was talking shit. He'd always grab the other person's shoulder when he talked. I knew him, and I knew that things were about to go south. I quickly jumped in front of Suge and pushed Puffy. I was like, "Get off my daddy." Suge knew I had heart, and had his back. And Puff's security couldn't do nothing because we had the whole V.I.P. surrounded. After all that commotion, we ended up going downstairs to party.

Chapter 11: New York, New York

After we left NY, I kept in contact with Mary. I flew back to NY to be with her more than five times after the awards. We had chemistry and the conversation was good. If I didn't love my girl so much, we would have really been on something serious.

The next time I flew into New York, my flight stopped for a layover before I got to Rochester. I was flying in to work with Devante Swing of Jodeci. When she found out that I was at the airport, she came and picked me up. She wanted to go and get something to eat, and spend some time with me before I left. I ended up missing my flight, but that was part of her plan; she had already booked a room.

When we got to the room, she was drunk as hell. That was another reason I couldn't get with her on some real shit. Soon as we hit the room, she ran and got in the shower. When she was done showering, she came out the bathroom with nothing on but a hotel shower robe. She had a glass of

Champagne in her hand and the bottle under her arm. She got in the bed and proceeded to go down on me. I was laid back on the bed, smoking the good green that she had gotten for me. She was stroking me with her mouth while I smoked. Boy, I was hooked. She told me that even though she was on her period, she still wanted to have sex. Initially, I was grossed out. But I smashed that ass anyway. It was messy, and there was blood everywhere! It looked like a scene of "Murder was the Case." It was so bad that me and Bloody Mary ended up changing rooms.

In the morning, she woke up and arranged for a car service to pick me up so that I could go to Rochester to work with Devante. When I got there, Devante sent some of his people to the airport to pick me up. When we got to the studio, Devante was sitting at the keyboard playing. He got up and ran over to me and gave me a hug and said, "Nigga, welcome to The Basement." There, he introduced me to Missy Elliott and her group, Sista, and to Static and his group,

Playa; Timbaland and Magoo, and Ginuwine. We listened to a lot of music that night, and even chilled for a minute. After the session, I took a Town Car and checked in at the hotel.

When I woke up, I wanted to go to the mall. I still had about five to six thousand dollars left from what Suge had given me. I called up Ginuwine to show me where the mall was. We shopped our ass off. We spent everything but $60. It was a good thing that Suge called to check on me. I told him that I was good, but he would always ask me if I had money. I told him that I did. When he asked how much, I had to hurry up and make up a number cause I hated asking him outright for money. I told him I had like $2K.

He clicked over on the office phone and told Roy, his assistant, to get $5K over to me. Within the hour, I was standing at Western Union picking up the money. We had to put some in other people's name because I had received more than the allowed amount.

Back at the studio, Devante played a song called "Slip and Slide" and another song called "It's All About You." An hour later, we were recording, and Ginuwine and I were both laying backgrounds for the song. It took me about four days to record the lead vocals. By that time, Ginuwine and I had become friends; we bonded like brothers. Even when I went back home, we made sure we kept in touch with each other.

We would always keep each other encouraged. I remember when some things popped off for him and he didn't know what move to make, we prayed together. I told him, after we prayed, that when you get these types of opportunities, you have to respond to them the right way, especially if where you are, and what you are doing isn't working. I wanted the music to happen for him. I really loved this dude. He was one of the realest people I had met. He came to LA a couple of times and I brought him to the studio to give him a little taste of Death Row and how we kicked it.

The next time that I saw him was when his video "Pony" premiered.

I was so happy for him. Even though he was separating from Devante, I still celebrated him. After all the praying and tears, he was finally where he wanted to be, and the world was going crazy over him.

When I returned to LA, I went directly to Suge's house; I wanted to play the songs for him. He immediately fell in love with "Slip and Slide." Every time we got together and talked about the song or the video, he would say, "You got to do this on the water, in the ocean." He'd ask me, "Can you walk on water?"

Chapter 12: Mother's Day Without Her

Needless to say, losing my mother wasn't something I could get over. It was tough to deal with the loss. So when I got the call from Suge to be a part of what would become an annual Mother's Day event, I was a bit apprehensive. But when Suge called, I answered.

We were going to perform and feed a thousand women and children at the Beverly Hills Hilton ballroom. K.C. and Jo-Jo, The Isley Brothers, Michel'le, Jewell and I were scheduled to perform. With the circumstances being what they were, I sang as much as I could. It was my very first Mother's day without my mom. I was feeling sad, but I wanted to do it for my mother. And I did just that. But immediately after I performed, I went backstage and cried my head off.

I was excited to be a part of a show that was giving back. It was a good thing to see Suge taking care of people he didn't even know. I mean, it was a Red Carpet event, and there were real stars performing. Some of the families were picked up by limos. Everyone that came left with a small Death Row medallion, and all of the mothers were given elaborate gift baskets.

After the show was done, we went back to the Peninsula Hotel and hung out with all of the performing artists. We chilled and drank, and drank and chilled all night. I couldn't believe that I was hanging with the Isley's and K.C. and Jo-Jo. I mean, these were the people I grew up listening to. What was once a lofty childhood dream was now reality. It was Death Row that made it happen, and I was immensely grateful!

Hanging out with my childhood idols was the highlight of the event, but little did I know, there were more surprises to come. Suge walked into my room and threw a black box at me. "Check this out D.B. and tell me if you like it," he said. I opened the box to see a large gold chain and a medallion. When I removed the cover from the medallion, it read "Danny" with the boy symbol under it. The chain looked as if it had millions of diamonds in it. I was so thrilled when I saw the piece. Suge just walked away smiling; he enjoyed giving gifts.

Two days later, Suge called me to his office. I took my time because Suge was known to show up five hours late. When I got there, I was three hours late and Suge still hadn't made it to the office. I waited there until I grew tired. Just as I was about to leave, somebody got of the elevator and said Suge was on his way up.

We talked for about thirty minutes before Suge asked me to walk down with him to go see my car. I jumped up immediately. When we got on the elevator all I could do was watch with anticipation as the numbers on the elevator got lower.

When the doors opened, I turned the corner to see my new, red, two-door car. I didn't know what kind of car it was. All I knew was that it was a two-door drop top. Come to find out, it was a Nissan, but it didn't matter what kind of car it was. Suge had customized the black interior with red accents. My name was embroidered on each of the floor mats: "Danny" on the driver's side and "Boy on the passenger side. I quickly jumped into the car and turned up the radio. I couldn't believe my life! Suge gave me a hug, got in his car, and drove off. I could tell that he was just as happy as I was. I was singing *Thank You* as Suge rode off. I hit the 101 for about an hour bumping oldies before I went to the crib and grabbed my girl; we rode all night.

Chapter 13: From Prison to Death Row

Early one morning, Suge called and asked me to meet him at the airport in Van Nuys. He told me to be there in an hour. I made sure that I got there before that hour was up. I only took a small overnight bag with me. He didn't tell me where we were going, and I didn't ask. When we boarded the jet, we flew about five hours before we landed in New York.

After we landed, we jumped into a late model limousine. We drove for several hours before we finally stopped at restaurant near Riker's Island. Suge sent me inside to get some food while he took a meeting at the prison. I sat in that restaurant nearly two hours before he returned.

When he re-emerged, the limousine driver took us back to the city. He didn't directly communicate the details of the meeting, but I overheard him talking on the phone. He was making plans to bring Tupac on board. He had been with Interscope, but when he went to prison, many in the industry gave up on him. Suge knew that Tupac was special, and he was determined to sign him to Death Row. He went back to visit Tupac a few more times before his release.

On the day of his release, I sat at the same restaurant waiting for Suge to return. But there was no indication that this visit was any different from the others. It wasn't until the limo pulled up that I realized that Pac had been released. It was October of 1995. Suge, David Kenner, Pac, and I were on our way back to California.

While we rode, Pac was flowing verses, smoking, and drinking. Suge had me singing oldies, like he always did. This time, Pac joined in. He kept requesting songs, and I kept singing. Even when I didn't know the song, I always knew the chorus.

When we finally arrived at the small, private airport, we pulled right up to the steps of a luxury jet. I had sung just about all of the old school songs I knew. As the stewardess waited at the top of the stairs, the driver unloaded our luggage. As soon as I got on the plane, I could see women everywhere. Some were half-naked with their breasts hanging out. The others had nothing on but thongs or boy shorts. It was one of the best flights I had ever been on. The girls danced, and we drank and smoked all the way to Los Angeles. I was truly enjoying flying the friendly skies. It was on that trip that I received my membership to the Mile High Club!

"Welcome to the city of stars," the captain said as we prepared to land. By the time we arrived, we couldn't wait to get off that long ass flight. You could see the look of excitement that Pac had on his face. It was obvious that he was happy to be out.

When we got to the gate, the limos were waiting to pick us up. I got in a Town Car and went to the crib to see my girl. Once I showered, and got dressed, I headed to the studio. Everybody was there waiting to see Pac, but he hadn't arrived. After several hours, I saw Kelvin Lewis running to the back door. As soon as Pac got out of the limo, he took about two steps and then, BAM! He fell straight on his face.

He had passed out, and they were putting water on his face trying to get him to come to. Between the flight and whatever else he did in between, he had overdone himself. It took about thirty minutes before they could get Pac up on his feet. Once he was able to walk on his own, he went right into the studio and started listening to tracks and writing. After that day, you could barely get him to do anything else.

If anyone wanted to talk to Pac or interview him, they had to come to Can-Am, because that's where he was working. This was the time when a lot of other celebrities came around Death Row. I had seen a lot of them on the red carpet events, but never in our studio. I saw artists like Queen Latifah, Treach and E40.

Pac's crew was called The Outlaws. They were like his protégés. He was grooming them—preparing them for the industry. They were with him every day. To be in Pac's presence was like sitting in a classroom, and the Outlaws were always in attendance. They were on point and had his back as much as he had theirs. I could appreciate their loyalty and truly admired them.

Pac had a constant stream of visitors after he was released. There were magazines, and other media, and even other artists in the industry. Faith was one of the first to show up with gifts. When she pulled up in her limo, she was wearing a hooded jogging suit, a hat, and sunglasses. I guess she was trying to move around incognito, but there was no hiding that bright blonde hair. I was laying in Suge's office watching her on the camera. She had about five runners bringing out boxes from her trunk. They were full of expensive clothes and items from Louis Vuitton. And they were all for Pac. At that time, Faith was still married to Biggie, and she had just dropped about forty grand on Pac. That's why I say that the whole East Coast versus West Coast shit had a lot to do with women.

We were all in the studio chilling when Pac got on the mic to record "Wonder Why They Call You Bitch." She went into the booth and laid the background vocals and ad-libs. When we headed back to the hotel, Faith stayed at the studio with Pac.

The song was fire, but her vocals couldn't be used. Her record label would not approve her appearance due to the beef that Biggie and Pac had going on. People were tripping over the fact that Biggie's wife was on Pac's shit.

When she was there, she stayed right under Pac. When he left, she left with him. Faith came around a lot, and it appeared that she and Pac were good friends from the outside looking in, but us on the inside knew that they had something more than that—something intimate. It wasn't a secret that she and Pac were fucking.

Chapter 14: All Eyez on Him

Pac was glowing. He was living the life of the rich and famous for the first time. Each day things got better for him. Hype was being built up about him being released from prison and signing to Death Row. Before Pac came to Death Row, he wasn't wearing a lot of jewelry. But once he signed, Suge started designing his pieces. This was a big deal because it was a sign that he was in. There was a clear difference between Pac's swag in the "Dear Mama" video and the ones that followed. Before long, Suge presented Pac with a car just like he did me. But this time, instead of a red two-door drop-top Nissan, it was a Black drop-top Benz with a red bow around it. Pac was elated!

As nice as it was to have Pac around, it also seemed to slow down production of my own record. I felt like Suge was putting my project on the backburner. Everything was about Pac and his album. Perhaps it was because I was his son that he felt that he could easily put my project on hold, but I wasn't the only one that felt like they were being sidelined. There was always someone who took priority over the other artists. Before Pac, there was Snoop. It was the nature of the beast.

While people had their different feelings about things, they couldn't deny the spirit Pac had. He was all about bringing people together. He tried to make sure everyone was involved.

Sometimes I would be in my room recording, and Pac would come in. "Danny Boy, come pop something on this track. Let me see what you come up with," he would say. This is how songs like "What's Your Phone Number," "Picture Me Rolling," "Heaven Ain't Hard to Find," "I Ain't Mad at Cha," and many more of our collaborations came to be.

Pac helped everyone's work ethic become better. He was constantly laying hit after hit. We knew that when we came out with something, we had to match his quality.

Everybody was trying to show Suge that they were stars. It became a friendly competition, because we really couldn't hate on Pac. He was the shit and everybody knew it. If you were a part of Death Row, you were going to be involved with what Pac was doing, some kind of way. Pac knew that the spotlight was on him, but I'm so grateful he let us shine with him.

Suge's artist roster proved that he was unstoppable. And he took care of us. We all had nice cars, the finest jewelry, and women at our disposal. But no matter how hard we played, we worked even harder. Making hits at Can-Am studios was so fulfilling that it didn't feel like work.

Me, Suge, and Pac were always together. And even our ladies rolled together. I remember us chilling at The Beverly Hills hotel with Faith, Misa, and Mary J. We were cool like that. But when it was time to work, we were on it. Pac always got to the studio very early in the morning, and sometimes wouldn't come out until the next day. Dude had a strong work ethic and it was paying off. He had all of the attention. Everything was revolving around him.

Most of that time, Suge maintained that my record was coming out next. But before long, he would change his tune. It wasn't for lack of me trying. I would be recording in Studio A while Pac was recording in Studio B. It wasn't Pac's fault though. I was glad that he was there. Every time Pac needed vocals, he would come in and put me on the track. I would be running back and forth between my room and Pac's room. I was singing on everything. Some of the stuff we did, I thought wouldn't fly, but to my surprise, the world loved it!

One night we were in the studio recording and the secretaries were all up on top of the tables dancing and stripping. We were drinking and Pac was talking shit on the mic. Pac called me in the booth, and we went off on this beat from one of Morris Day's songs. We took it and made it our own. That's how we came up with "What's Your Phone Number." It was a crazy session. We drank and smoked all night. I think this was the longest song we recorded on the "All Eyez On Me" album.

We recorded our vocals and then kept the mic on in the room and let it record for hours. Everything on the record was organic and real. There was audio of Pac talking shit to the girls, ad-libbing, and laughing; it was all live. We recorded right into the early morning.

That same week, we were scheduled to have a photo shoot with Vibe Magazine. Pac, Suge, and Snoop were on the cover. The rest of the artists came in one by one and had their photos taken. We all had on black shirts. I didn't like the idea of wearing the same shirts. I thought the idea was corny, but once I saw the layout, I changed my mind. Any doubts I had went away real fast. Pac was taking Death Row to another level, and we all were going with him.

Dr. Dre was the co-owner of Death Row at this time, but he was rarely present. It was hard to get him to come in on a session. It didn't matter to him that you were an artist on the same label. That guy wasn't working with you unless he wanted to. His head was in production, and for most of us, he wasn't accessible. He'd only work with a certain type of artist. Out of all the years I was on the label, I may have been in the same studio with him once or twice.

Pac was always tripping to Suge about Dre. He felt that Dre wasn't really down with Death Row and that he was distant with everyone. It just took too much to get Dre in the studio. Suge was saying that Dre was pissed because he chose to put "California Love" on Pac's "All Eyez On Me" album. For that, and probably other reasons, Suge and Dre's relationship was deteriorating; they just couldn't see eye to eye.

They could have also been having a little tiff because Suge was creeping with Michel'le, Dre's girlfriend and baby mama. Suge could be messy at times—like saying that Dre was gay, and that he caught him in bed with a man. I think Dre was over that bullshit. It wasn't long before Dre left

Death Row. He left the label without asking for a dime. He had partnership in Death Row; he owned a percentage. What that percentage was, I don't know, but he didn't give a damn.

Dre might have left his share, and his rights to Death Row; but he still had his sound. If a record was whack, Dre could turn it into a hit.

He had to start from the bottom again. Things started off kind of shaky for him in the beginning, but he got it together. In no time, he introduced the world to Eminem. Eminem brought 50 Cent to the table, and 50 brought G-Unit.

After Dre left Death Row, Pac started making diss albums toward him. With Pac and Suge being like brothers, they did everything together. If Pac had a problem, Suge adopted the problem and vice versa.

Chapter 15: "All Eyez On Me Tour"

When we left California for a couple of spot dates, our first stop was Cleveland, Ohio. Just about all of the artists on the label went on the road with Pac: Snoop, Tha Dogg Pound, Michel'le, The Outlaws, OFTB, and a few other artists. We didn't go anywhere without the homies with us. It was a good time, but by sound check, we were all smashed.

When Michel'le came out onto the stage, she was supposed to ride out on a three-wheeled bike. She came riding the bike from behind the stage and completely rode off of the ramp that she was on. We cracked up laughing. Well, after we helped her up. She was lucky that it was a ramp and not a high stage, or else she would have been singing a whole other tune.

On the way back to the hotel, it was snowing heavily. The radio station was reporting a snowstorm. We were literally walking in snow that came up to our knees. We thought the show might be cancelled, or that few people would come out, but the fans showed up. They were determined to see Pac!

When Pac and The Outlaws hit the stage, the crowd went crazy! But before Pac started his second song, somebody had thrown a crutch up onto the stage. Pac told the DJ to stop the music. "I'll give $5,000 to the person who'll tell me who threw it," Pac said to the crowd. Man, it had to be about 5,000 people pointing in the same direction. Pac threw a wad of money into the crowd, and the homies snatched the dude up out of there quicker than you could blink your eye. That dude probably don't do shit now, but go to jazz concerts.

The next morning we were on our way to the next city. When we got to the airport, flights were being pushed back because of the weather. After some hours, we finally boarded our flight. Everything was fine until we had to sit on the runway for another hour.

I went into my bag and pulled out two fifths of Crown Royal. I was passing it out when one of the stewardesses tried to catch us up, but I was the only one that got caught with my drink out. The stewardess saw me and said, "Sir, you can't bring drinks aboard this plane."

We were on our way down the runway when I started going off on her. She made a phone call, and the next thing I knew, they were turning the plane around. We were headed back to the gate. About five police and sheriffs got on the plane. "Young man in the red sweater, come to the front of the plane," they said.

When I stood up, our publicist, George Price, walked up to talk to them. If George hadn't stepped up, I think they would have locked me up. Instead, they made us all get off the plane. Everybody was mad at me because it was the last flight of the night. We had to wait until the next day to get a flight and that meant we would be sleeping in the halls of the terminal until it was time to go.

They were hot as hell, but they knew they couldn't say nothing to me or they were going to have a problem with Suge. And if Suge had a problem, the big homies would solve it. Ain't nobody have time for the big homies. I felt bad, but I continued to put my arrogance on full display. I kept laughing and talking shit in as I walked through the halls of the terminal.

We went to several other cities and did some shows at smaller venues. During this time, "All Eyez On Me" was being mixed and mastered. When we returned to LA, Pac went to the desert to shoot the "California Love" video. It was directed by his friend, Jada Pinkett-Smith. Interscope and Death Row were preparing to release it. They had a big campaign and promotion going on.

Shortly after the filming of the video, Suge, Pac, The Outlaws and some more of us went back to New York for Pac's appearance on Saturday Night Live. I ended up finding out that I was going to be singing with Pac. It was the first time I was actually scared to sing.

All I could hear on the production speakers was, "Countdown…we're going live in 5,4,3,2,1." We barely made it out of wardrobe before they were pushing us out toward the stage. When the lights came on, people were clapping. Pac was going hard. I was sitting with Big Syke on the stage behind Pac.

When it was my turn, I was trying to stay in the background—not trying to do too much, but Syke was like, "Gone D." Then Pac fumbled over one of parts in the verse, and I came in to help him, *I ain't mad at cha*, I sang. After he did his next verse, he put me on. "This is seventeen-year-old Danny Boy from Chicago," he said. He shined his light on me in that moment. I had his back, and he had mine. I was still scared, but I did my best to represent.

I was finally starting to feel like a celebrity. All of my family was back in Chicago watching me perform live. My grandmother even let my little cousins stay up late to see it, and she watched it with them. I never saw my grandmother watch anything other than Rev. Clay Evans or TBN. I was satisfied enough just to know that she was watching me. That was large in itself.

Chapter 16: Slip & Slide

After putting in so much work in the studio, it was finally time for me to see the treatment for the "Slip & Slide" video. They presented storyboards explaining the concept of the video. They were impressive, but the kicker was the location: Cabo San Lucas, Mexico! Suge put a lot of money into this shoot. He was dead set on his vision of me walking on water. It would require a large piece of Plexiglas suspended over the ocean. There was little time to prepare. I had to rush my passport application in order to leave on time.

The following week, Trina and I were working to get everything at the house in order. Our nanny was going to be staying at our house to care for Ashley while we were away in Mexico. We quickly hosted a casting call to find my leading lady and a few extras. We ended up choosing about eighty girls. In preparation for the shoot, I met with the wardrobe stylist. She pulled some nice looks for the shoot. She even had custom underwear with my name on them.

When it was time to leave, Death Row had two airplanes full of our people. Now, that doesn't even count the private flights that brought 2Pac, Snoop, Tha Dogg Pound, Nate Dogg, DJ Quik, K-Ci and JoJo, Aaron Hall and whoever else they wanted to bring. That was how we rolled. You brought your people with you.

Suge, David Kenner, Michel'le, Trina and I flew in on a small passenger jet. We were eating, chilling and listening to music when we landed at the airport in Mexico. We arrived to police escorts, who took me and my girl to our villa. Suge had rented a big house that he and Michel'le stayed in. David Kenner stayed on his boat. My stylist flew in with about $50K worth of clothes, but she neglected to declare their value to customs, and they confiscated everything. My clothes, my shoes and everything she had customized for me was gone too.

She had to turn around and go back to the States and grab whatever she could to make the shoot. It was tight because we would be filming the next afternoon. Boy, when you have money, you can make just about anything happen. She was back just in time for me to do my thing. The first scenes we shot were in the jungle.

After that first scene, my girl went off on me because she thought I was doing too much with my leading lady. I was kissing and grinding on her, but that was part of the performance. The next day, I left her at the Villa with my assistant while I shot my scenes.

The next scene was the one with me on water. " You'll walk out in the middle of the water, do a little dancing and walk towards the camera," the director said to me. I didn't have a problem with that. It seemed easy; except for the dancing part. I wasn't much of a dancer. I was cool throughout the entire makeup and hair sessions, but when they told me I'd have to take a dingy out to the location, I started to rethink the entire scene. The distance was too far, and I couldn't swim. I wasn't having it. It took the crew twenty minutes to assure me that everything would be okay. When my makeup and hair stylist and I got on the dingy with the driver, I had my life jacket on under my actual jacket.

There were scuba divers swimming around the sides of the Plexiglas just in case I fell in. They didn't have to worry about me falling in, because I had no intention of getting out of the boat. I was scared. Some of the guys eventually helped me out of the boat. When I stood on the Plexiglas, it moved. I felt like I was about to have a heart attack. I started encouraging myself…*I'm good. I got this.*

Once I got up the courage to stand up in the middle of the water, the director yelled, "Have Danny Boy take off the life jacket. It's making him look too bulky!" When he said that, I wanted to change my mind about singing, because they wanted me to take the vest off and get off the dingy. Shit! That was my protection. I wasn't dying that day for nothing and nobody.

Finally, the divers came to me and explained that they would be swimming along the edges of the Plexiglas. With that assurance, I went ahead and gave them all the shots they needed. Now that it's all said and done, I think that it was a stupid scene. It was a great concept, but I should have never let them convince me to dance. It was money wasted. We should have just cut the scene. What makes it even worse is…I actually look like I can't dance.

I was walking on water; just like Suge said I would. But I didn't care anymore. I just wanted to get off of that boat, and get back to land. Later that night, we shot a scene on a submarine. It was a real submarine too. We had to climb on top in order to get in. We were floating on water and then all of the sudden we were underwater. I was at the window looking at how deep we were going. I can see all kinds of fish and things swimming around that I had never seen in my life, not even on TV.

The next morning, we ate breakfast at Suge's rental house while the maids were at the Villa cleaning. My boy, Kurt Cobain and my friend, Troy were flying in to hang with me. The production van took me to pick them up from the airport. I had known Troy since Orr. I'd met Kurt one day when I was leaving the studio. He had told me that he produced records. When we were leaving one day, I noticed that he was sleeping in his truck. It was broken down, and he couldn't get it started. He told me that he ran out of money, and that he had been sleeping in his truck for the last week. I didn't know him man from Adam, but I put him and Troy in my car, and welcomed them into our home. We'd been friends from that day on. I was happy to have Kurt and Troy with me in Cabo.

After I picked up my boys, we headed back to the video set in Mexico. When we pulled up to the set, the streets were blocked off. The driver said to the guards "This is Danny Boy." After that, they let us in immediately.

We finished shooting early that day, because everybody was going to meet up at the club to celebrate the video, and the success of Pac's album. We rented every scooter, golf cart and dune buggy they had in Cabo. We got in the club and were partying and everything was going smooth. We had the bar tied down. We bought the bar out and it was open to any and everybody in there. There were so many people, most I didn't recognize. There were like forty Crips, and sixty Bloods—two rival gangs in one place? I knew something bad was going to happen. The locals probably had never seen that many niggas at once.

Suge and I were standing by the door talking to some of the big homies when an older lady made a smart remark to one of Suge's homies. The guy just started banging on that lady. It was obvious that he had never been further than Vegas; he slapped that lady right off her feet. While she was on the floor, he was yelling at her, "Bitch, get up! I dare you. This Piru, get up!" he said, screaming his gang's name. The other big homies had to come get him off of her. They quickly rushed him and took him out of the bar. I don't think he even realized just how fast the authorities would lock him up.

Over the next few days, we shot more scenes. On our last day of shooting, we were on Suge's boat, *P Funk*. It was hard to concentrate on the scene because every girl on the boat was topless. All I could think about was the after party.

The final scene of the night was a party scene. I hadn't realized how many people Suge had flown down until I pulled up and got off the golf cart. Everywhere I looked, people were standing. It looked like a huge ass block party. All of the people that flew on the private jet had people with them: Pac, Snoop, Tha Dogg Pound, D.J. Quik, and OFTB; it looked like a scene in Boyz In The Hood.

The leading lady and I had to take off everything that we had on, jewelry and all. The camera would pan across the sand to give the illusion that we were somewhere having sex.

They were shooting that scene at one end of the beach, and she and I were shooting at the other end. When the producers yelled, "Wrap!" the entire crew was happy to be done. The video had taken a week and a half to shoot; it was time to celebrate!

I hadn't seen my boys, Troy and Kurt since earlier that day. My assistant, Dion had taken off with my camera and was having his own little photo shoot. "Can you snap this for me right quick?" he'd ask random people. I didn't have one picture on my camera for memories. Death Row had their photographer take pictures, but I never had the opportunity to see them   either.

When I went back to pick up my jewelry, I noticed that the assistant director was looking around like he had lost something. In fact, everyone was looking nervous. That made me nervous because nobody was walking up to me handing me my jewelry.

Dion walked up to the director and started cursing at him about my shit. Then I started going off on him. "Why in the hell weren't you being an assistant and watching my shit?" I asked him, "You are here to assist. My job is to do what I'm doing, and your job is to do what I need you to do!"

I was mad as hell because my watch, chain and two rings had vanished. I had lost nearly $30K in jewelry. I was so mad that I made the guy that was driving the cart get off. I drove off and left Dion standing right there with him.

An hour later, Suge pulled up in this van and asked to me, "Danny Boy, who got yo shit, Blood?" I was looking crazy, he was looking crazy, and he had about a hundred homies with him. He got out of the van and we all started mobbing toward the area where my jewelry was. Everybody saw that Suge was coming and that he was pissed off. The homies started checking everybody that didn't walk up with us. I looked around and Dion, my so-called assistant, was nowhere to be found.

Suge walked up to Troy and Kurt. As soon as he walked up, he got in Troy's face. He said to Troy and Kurt, "You niggas ain't never been nowhere for real! Danny Boy gave y'all the opportunity to come, and he treating y'all to everything and neither one of y'all helped keep up with his shit? His shit missing, and y'all got to pay for it!" I knew Suge wasn't talking about money because they didn't have shit. They were living off of me; I was taking care of them. These were my people. Troy was skinny as hell, probably weighed no more than 100 pounds. He was shaking and apologizing, "I'm sorry Mr. Knight."

Kurt was high as hell, and when Suge got in his face, he smirked. Somebody out of the crowd reached over and hit Kurt in the mouth. Blood was everywhere. He was in a daze, and scared as hell. "This some bullshit! So you gone do my people like this?" I said as Suge was holding me. Pac and Hammer were grabbing Troy and Kurt. Pac said, "Danny Boy, you want somebody to check they people when they out

119

of order, but you ain't saying that now because it's your people." I told Pac to shut his ass up. We were friends, but this wasn't the way to handle things.

Pac and Suge had Troy's little ass standing in between them. They started asking Troy, "Who look like they been working out?" Troy was scared to answer because he knew that regardless of who he picked, the other one was going to be on some bullshit! Hammer was by the sink jumping around like he was in a boxing ring, putting on the gloves with the fingertips out.

"We gone fuck him up if Danny Boy don't," Suge said laughing. I thought Troy was about to get a beat down until Suge said to me, "You take care of your people, or we will!" Troy was crying. He looked at me and said, "Danny Boy, Please, you do it."

I made it look like I punched Troy in his chest, but what I really did was push him really hard with my fist. That was enough for Suge and Pac. They walked away and Hammer followed behind them.

When Troy got up off the floor, he ran to me and gave me a hug. I wasn't going to let them hurt my boy. I wasn't worried about Kurt. He was standing outside with a swollen lip.

When I got back to my Villa, Dion wasn't there. I didn't think he had the jewelry, but he was still in violation for spending $7K on a private flight back to LA. He got out of there fast, because he was scared of getting his ass whopped in Mexico.

Chapter 17: Scared to Fly

After that eventful night, it was time for everyone to go home. Suge, David Kenner, Michel'le, Trina and I stayed behind an extra week. We went out on a boat to do some fishing. Suge and I even caught a shark. When we pulled that big fellow onto the boat, that thing was jumping around everywhere.

We rode late into the night with our girls and the captain of P-funk. I had gotten so drunk that I woke up the next morning not knowing how I got back to the Villa. It was early in the morning, and we were up packing getting ready to head to the airport. It was the weekend, so the airport closed early.

Suge was taking his time as usual. By the time we pulled up to the airport, every light in there was going off. Suge ran up to the door to talk to the people inside. About five to ten minutes later, he came to the car and said, "Don't

trip. They gone let us in. I gave them a couple of dollars."
Classic Suge. The man could make things happen.

After we boarded the plane, we sat on the runaway for about 20 minutes before we took off. I was sitting in the back with Trina and Michel'le; Suge and David Kenner were sitting together. The blues were playing loudly, and they were smoking cigars. I was passing my blunt back and forth to David Kenner. We were singing, joking and having a good time like we always did. Just as the captain announced that we were free to move around, we hit an air pocket that jerked the plane a little. We were accustomed to turbulence, but this was a little more rough than usual. As the plane began to drop, it got harder to hear what people were saying.

David looked out of the window in panic. "The plane is on fire!" he shouted. "Land this motherfucker!" At this point, we were falling hundreds of feet per minute. Trina had fainted; she was out cold. And I was crying, praying, and quoting every scripture I had learned since I was a kid.

As we continued to fall, the pilot did everything he could to regain control. He was working the plane—swaying it from side to side. I could see the flames coming from the wing; I started hyperventilating. Suge grabbed me. With a cigar in his mouth, he promised me that God loved us. He told me that we're going be okay because we still had work to do. And he was right. It was not our time.

When we landed, police, ambulances, and fire trucks were all over the runway. Suge was right, we should've been dead. They should have been looking for a group of black bodies and a little black box, but God had it all planned differently.

As soon as I realized that we had landed, I was at the door trying my best to tear it off. I swear I thought that I would become a citizen of Mexico, because I didn't ever see myself getting on another plane. I didn't wait for anyone to help me. I just ran off the plane and started praising God like never before. I was thankful to God for sparing my life.

The next morning, we arrived at the airport on time. The only thing that made me feel okay about getting on it was that flight was that we would be on a big, commercial plane. As we prepared for takeoff, I said a prayer. We had a long way to go. It was hard for me to keep in together. I was constantly watching the time. When we were finally on approach, I started singing my head off. I couldn't wait to be home. In fact, I was standing up as we taxied toward gate.

Trina and I went straight to the house to get to Ashley. We had been so close to never seeing her again. When we arrived home, we ran upstairs to see her. This was one of the few times in a long time that Trina and I got along. From that day on, we kept Ashley really close to us.

Once we settled down, I slept for a few hours. Then it was time to get back to the studio. I stayed until five in the morning. On my route home, I had to drive over a mountain. All I remember is getting to the bottom, and then nothing. When I woke up, I was under a semi-truck. Blood was coming from my head, and I could hear D'Angelo's "Brown Sugar" bumping in the background. I jumped out of the car and called up to the office to tell them what had happened. They immediately got Suge on the phone to talk to me. I was scared as hell, because the car was still new. It only had about 1400 miles on it.

Suge asked me if I was okay. He told me to go to the hospital, and to stop by the studio when I was done. I was in and out in about three hours. When I was done, I went straight to the studio, neck-brace and all. When I got there, Snoop and everybody was making fun of me. I waited around all night for Suge to arrive. When he got there, he just laughed and told me that he was glad I was okay. "Don't trip about the car," he said. I went home and stayed there for four days. The pain was bad.

After being down for so many days, I went back to the lab in a rental car the studio had leased for me. It was a green Ford Taurus—a sad substitute for my red drop-top. It wasn't the flash that I'd become accustomed to, but I had just shot a million-dollar video, I was on one of the most anticipated albums of the year, and Suge had assured me that my project was next. There was nothing to complain about.

Chapter 18: Toss It Up

As Death Row was on the rise, a group of industry veterans began to speak out against what they called, Gansta Rap. Dionne Warwick, Diana Ross, and Delores Tucker were very vocal about what they felt were the negative impacts of this type of music. In essence, they were messing with Suge's money, and that wasn't a good thing. Their "campaign" had begun to cause problems with distribution. Suge surely didn't want anything to affect Pac's album. So he decided to meet with Dionne at her Hollywood home. He wanted to see if they could find some middle ground. But Delores wanted money, and that's where things stalled. The conversation had started out calm, but things soon escalated, and Suge ended up cussing Dionne out.

It was around this time that I met Michael Jackson for the first time. I was excited, to say the least. It wasn't unusual for Suge to take me along for meetings. This was Suge's training ground. He would put us in front of the giants, and demand that we stay composed. There were no photos or shaking hands unless it was initiated by the other person. So when Michael extended his hand, I was more than happy to oblige. Suge wanted him to do a Christmas record with me. He had heard "I Ain't Mad At Cha," and he liked it! "That's some Dope Shit!" he said. It was crazy. Michael Jackson was saying that our music was Dope! At that point, it didn't matter what anyone else said, MJ had heard by vocals, and he was impressed!

With Pac's album done, Death Row and Interscope were deep into promotion. They had the world waiting on his album to drop. While I was excited for the world to hear me on Pac's album, I was anxious for my own record to be released. One thing was certain, it was going to be an interesting journey. There were many interviews and appearances, but the kicker was the spread we did for Vibe magazine. When that issue came out, I got calls from my family and friends all across the world. I really felt like a star.

Over the years, I had become a fixture in the music community. Being Suge Knight's son didn't hurt either. And while I had formed many friendships, a small group of my LA homies and I had committed to having each other's backs. I decided that we would call ourselves, Kommittee. It was a brotherhood similar to that of a fraternity. The members included Ray J, Young Buck, Short Mac, Sean Young, Siggy Jackson, Chris Buck, and I. The older members would guide the younger ones, and we would make sure that none of us was left without support. That was the promise we made to one another.

We spent a lot of time at Ray J's house. I never told him, but I had the biggest crush on Brandy. But Ray J was sure to keep her at a distance. We would be in one room, and she would be in another. None of the homies had a chance with her. She was cool, though. She used to always ask to drive my car. I'd tell her, "You can't drive my car—Ask Wanya if you can drive his Benz." She was dating him at the time, but truth is, she could've had her way with me. I loved her.

My life in LA was vastly different from my childhood in Chi. There were new challenges each day, but there were also many surprises. A couple weeks after the Vibe shoot, me and some of the members of Kommittee were rolling down Sunset Boulevard high as hell when we looked up and saw the Vibe photo on the billboard. We rode down Sunset Boulevard at least once a week to see it and show it to the other homies.

During this time, I was still working on my project with the best producers and writers—Devante Swing, Portrait, the late Roger Troutman, the Underdogs and so many other great producers that later became very successful. After one of these productive sessions, I left the studio to see three brand-new Bentleys on three different flatbed trucks. I was charged up because I just knew that one of them was for me. There was a burgundy one that I knew was Suge's. The white one I thought was mine, and I was kind of confused because I didn't think he would get Pac blue one. It was always Suge, Pac, and Me—I just assumed that they were for us. But I was in for a surprise.

In no time, Snoop pulled up and jumped in the blue one. When Suge and Pac arrived, Pac got in one and Suge got in the other—neither one was for me. I was probably still too young for a Bentley, but I was jealous. But I got over it, and went back into the studio to work on some more music.

*****

We were in rehearsal for the Second Annual Mother's day event, and I was still mourning my mother. It was my second Mother's Day without her. This was the first year that Pac was going to be a part of the show. Everyone was excited about that. My cousin, Prez flew out to be with me during this time.

This is the same week that we shot the "I Ain't Mad at Cha" video. When Pac and I came out of the trailer, we were both tripping because a guy that looked just like Miles Davis walked right past us, and then a Redd Foxx look alike. It was the freakiest thing ever. We shot the video in two days. I was happy because it was just Pac and I on the song; it was my biggest feature to date.

The day of the Mother's day event, I woke up crying; I was so sad. Suge couldn't even stand to look at me in my face. Every time Suge looked at me, his eyes would well up. Pac tried too, but he ended up crying.

When they announced that it was my time to come up, the crowd went wild. After I finished my set, Suge came out and introduced Tupac; the crowd went crazy. When Pac hit the stage, the band was playing "Dear Mama." Pac spoke to the crowd and said, "While Danny Boy out here singing for y'all, he don't have *no* mama, and my home boy Mutah don't have a mother either." I was standing on the side of the stage crying, but what made me feel better was the glow on Pac's mom's face as he performed that song.

I had thought that the previous year's show was great, but this one was one of the best shows ever. Just like the year before, we passed out little gold Death Row medallions to all of the mothers, took pictures, and signed autographs. After the show was over, I went upstairs to my room, and cried myself to sleep.

Several weeks after the mother's day event, a group by the name of Black Street came out with a song called "No Diggity." Pac decided that we would go into the studio to record a song using the same beat, and that's what we did. K-Ci, JoJo, Aaron Hall, Tupac, and I came up with the song "Toss it Up." Working alongside these guys was incredible. We would have friendly singing competitions. It would be Aaron Hall against K-Ci, and JoJo against me. I was creating moments in my life that I would always remember.

After the studio session, I got a call from Suge. He told me to meet him at his house in Compton. Like always, I waited a while before I headed out. I called up one of the homies to ride out with me. When we got to his house, there were so many cars lined up on the street that it looked like there was a Blood fest going on.

We spent the day shooting pool, drinking, smoking, and just having a good time. After everyone left, Bountry and I stayed and shot some pool with Suge. He was killing me as usual.

When we finally got ready to leave, Suge came up to the gate, tossed me a set of keys, and walked off. I was wondering what he wanted me to do, I never knew with Suge. My homeboy was like, "Nigga, that's yo ride." I was running down the street looking and no one would even show me where the car was. I was pushing buttons, looking, and running. When I got halfway down the block, I saw it! It was an E320 Benz drop-top. It had peanut butter colored seats, a blacktop, and burgundy colored rims.

I was jumping, shouting, and crying. I still had that ugly green Ford Taurus rental car, so I gave those keys to my homie, and I hopped into my new Benz for the very first time. Every time I got to a traffic light, I let the top up and down. I sped all the way home from Compton Killings Street to Brentwood. When Trina came down to see the car, she was excited. We went and got some food and rode around all night. When I got home, we were pumping the music loud as hell.

The next morning, I received a notice and a fine for the loud music. This was around the same time as the O.J. Simpson trial and I lived right around the corner from the murder scene. I had actually watched from my rooftop as they cleaned up the crime scene.

Being that I was young and black, we were going to have a problem no matter what we did. It also didn't make it any better that when he was acquitted, I went and bought hundreds of dollars of orange juice and formed a caravan with my homies to pass out juice. It was a bad move on my part. Not long after, we were evicted.

When it was time to shoot the video for "Toss It Up," the team presented the idea of a party on the beach. We were supposed to find out about the party while we were on the plane. We would be ejected from the plane, and land at the party.

When we got to the set, we were all dressed in suits, but we were drunk as hell. Tupac and Suge were joking about Dre being gay, and about Bobby Brown getting his ass beat by JoJo. I was already mad about something else. When Pac saw my face, he said, "Danny Boy what you looking so sad for? You *gone* make Michael Jordan not want to play for the bulls no more!" Pac was a jokester. He was good at making me laugh. No one could be mad for long when they were in his presence.

When the video was completed, no one was really feeling it. We decided to shoot another video with a totally different concept. When we saw the new storyboards, we were excited! Within weeks, we were back in downtown Los Angeles getting ready to film the new video for "Toss It Up" with fine ass, Lisa Raye.

Pac had been promoting "All Eyez on Me" while working on the "Machiavelli 7 Day Theory" album. He was M.I.A., and no one could find him. He finally showed up just as they were about to cancel the whole shoot. He was more than five hours late when he arrived—walking in like George Jefferson. I was mad is hell, because I thought he was getting beside himself. When I saw Pac, I was cursing him out. "Shut up nigga,'" he said laughing. "This *my* video! Now let's get to work!"

Before the shoot, Aaron Hall had gotten locked up, so they pulled in an extra to play his role. The guy looked just like him, so nobody tripped. This version of the video was way better; the vibe was right. We filmed well into the early morning. After we wrapped, we all rode to Vegas to see the Mike Tyson vs. Bruce Sheldon fight.

Chapter 19: Vegas Nights

We rode from California to Vegas—forty cars deep. We were on our way to the Tyson fight. Right before we crossed the state line, we stopped at a restaurant. Some college dudes at the restaurant started talking crazy to Pac on some gang banging shit. They had no idea that there were a bunch of the homies outside. When one of the dudes came out of the restaurant, the homies rolled up on him. It was like a scene from an action movie. People were being knocked into their places for talking crazy to Pac. After the chaos, we all jumped in our cars and continued on our trip.

When we were about two hours away, one of the producers, Damon Thomas, had an accident and flipped his Viper over seven times. With so many cars in the caravan, we had no clue about the accident until we made it to Vegas.

When we got to Vegas, we checked into the Luxor Hotel. Later on that day we went to one of the other hotels to gamble. When we were on our way out, Pac noticed one of the guys that had tried to get his chain from one of the homies. His name was Orlando Anderson. Puffy had a bounty out for Death Row medallions, and he was paying $75K. The would-be thieves knew that they were going to have to hurt, or kill someone in order to get the chain. When Orlando realized that we knew who he was, he tried to run. That's when all hell broke loose. The fight was so big, and people were running from everywhere. The security guards ran toward us deep as hell, but they were too scared to come close to us. We rushed the exit, and left the building.

When we made it back to the hotel, we got dressed to head out to The Strip. It was always the best part of the trip. We would all dress up. It was like Suge was Tony Soprano, and we were his guys. I was almost dressed when Suge asked me to meet him and Pac downstairs.

I got on the elevator thinking I was clean as hell, but as soon as I got off, one of the hotel staff told me that there was something on the back of my pants. When I looked down, I couldn't tell if it was ketchup, hot sauce, coffee, or what; it was everywhere.

I told Suge that I needed to get some more clothes. I didn't want it looking like I had shitted on myself. Suge told me that I had better run over to the mall and grab something and then meet them at the fight. I took a cab over to the mall, but everything was closing early. I happened to find a store where I was able to replace my pants, but the problem was, their seamstress had already left for the day. I was always clean. There was no way I was showing up with unhemmed pants. I took a page out of The Grandmother's Playbook, and ran to Woolworth's to get some fabric tape. I went back to the room and ironed my pants. When I was done, they looked they had been custom tailored.

When I got in the car, I called Suge. He said to me, "Shit. You might as well go straight to the club. Tyson knocked this fool out in one round." When I arrived at Club 662, it was cracking. All of the A-listers were there. It was where Tyson came to party. People came out to Vegas just to come to Club 662—even if they didn't have tickets to the fight.

I had been at the club for about two hours when one of the homies came in and said, "Suge and Pac just got smoked on the strip!" I was tripping out. I immediately went into panic mode. Security was all over me trying to see where I was going. They were watching my every move.

When we got down to the strip, it was very crowded. People were everywhere. One of the homies chirped us and told that they were at the University Medical Center. Someone said that they had been killed. "They just been shot, they straight," another homie said. I didn't know what to believe. Suge was a father to me, and Pac was like a brother. I was inconsolable. My mind was on getting to the hospital; I had to see them for myself.

When I got there, everyone was in the emergency room. I was shaking and crying. I can't explain the feeling I had. I thought they were dead. We waited at the hospital until late into the night. Suge fared better than Pac. He ended up signing himself out of the hospital after suffering a graze to his head. Pac was in bad shape. When Suge went into Pac's room, and saw him on life support, I think he went into shock. It was a lot to take in. He was lost for words. His eyes were different. He was lost. Everyone left the hospital for the night and went back to the hotel. When we got back to the house in Vegas, Suge wanted everyone to leave; he wanted to be alone.

Tupac was like a little brother to Suge too. Ever since his release from jail, we had been inseparable. I was scared. I had been acting like this grown-ass man, but I was still a kid. I thought we were untouchable. Suge was like Superman to me. And now he was falling apart, I was falling apart, and Pac was on his deathbed.

We were just together laughing like we always would. All this flashed into my mind as I prayed for a miracle. I remembered how I would always try to beat Pac to the car whenever we were about to roll out somewhere. This dude and I used to play shotgun—whoever got there first would get the front seat; Pac always won. I would have to sit behind him because nobody could sit behind Suge.

At the hospital, the reporters and paparazzi were in full force. It seemed that they would do anything to get a story. They wanted the story so bad that they sent in young kids to listen and write about what was going on. Everyone in the camp had to become security at that point because we had to be sure that no one would be able to breach our security. We were sure to protect Pac against anyone who might want to bring more harm to him. We had to put people out left and right.

Pac was drifting away, but you couldn't even tell it, because Pac was a fighter. We expected him to pull through. None of us could imagine life, or Death Row without Pac.

As the days went by, people would call in threats to the hospital. They would say things like they knew where his bed was, and that they were going to come and finish the job. We ended up parking a U-Haul truck on the side of his room just to give him some kind of protection. He was on life support and could not be moved. We would take turns walking around the hospital, and if anything looked suspicious, we were on top of it.

Sometimes we would gather around Pac's mother and pray. One of those times, his mom asked me to sing. I sung one of the songs that he always liked to hear me sing: "*I was born by the river, in a little tent. Just like the river, I been running ever since. It's been a long, long time coming but I know, a change gone come.*" As I was singing, tears rolled down his face. I knew he had heard me. He knew that we were there in the room with him.

When we would ask Pac if he knew who we were, he would kick his feet. But perhaps it was our imagination. We wanted him to survive, but he was drifting away. We prayed and cried, and cried and prayed.

His mother was one of the strongest women I'd ever met. She would just smile and pray. "My baby is gone be all right," she'd say. On Pac's fifth day in the hospital, I went to pray for him. As I prayed and sung in his ear, he again shook his feet. I still had hope. I thought Pac was going to be okay. I stayed with him till the early morning.

Friday the 13th

I was sleeping in my room at the Luxor hotel after being at the hospital all night. I was awakened to the sound of hotel security and one of the homies banging on my door. It had to be about five o'clock in the morning. I opened my door in a panic. Pac was gone.

I ran down to valet, and as soon as I pulled out of the parking lot the radio station played, "I Shed So Many Tears." The fans were crying, the DJ was crying, I was crying, but I was still in doubt. *Pac can't be dead*, I thought.

When I pulled up at the hospital and saw thousands of people crying and holding up signs, I knew it was real. I jumped out in the middle of the street with the car still in drive. When I got to the door, the nurse was standing there waiting. "I'm sorry about Mr. Shakur, and sorry for your loss," she said. I fell right to the floor. Security picked me up and took me back to the hotel where everyone was meeting.

It felt like the world was standing still; everyone was in a daze. We were sitting around talking about arrangements when Afeni said, "I don't want nobody standing over him." She paced the floor back and forth for a while. And then she stopped, "Go on peacock. Spread your wings," she said. I can still hear her voice.

Afeni turned to us and said that she would make arrangements for Tupac to be cremated. I instantly threw up all over the floor where Suge was standing. It literally made me sick to my stomach to know that my brother's body would be cremated. I felt like Pac would have wanted his service to be like a concert. That's what the lyrics said,

"Have a party at my funeral, let every rapper rock it."

"Man, you know we have to go with what she wants," Suge said. Suge still didn't want to be around anybody. He had completely shut down. It was another one of the saddest days in entertainment history.

A few days after Pac's urn was delivered, the video director of "I Ain't Mad at Cha" sent Suge a version of the video. No one had ever seen the video besides the editors, not even Pac. I was sitting there watching this video where we were acting like we were in heaven. In the video, the Redd Foxx lookalike spoke to Tupac, saying, "Man, I been struggling trying try to get in here a long time. You gone have to earn your way. I sure hope you can make it."

At this point, I was just coming into adulthood. I was signed to a label called Death Row, and acting in a video where I'm acting out life after death. To know that Pac was gone, and that I was pretty much the only person in the video living; it felt like a premonition. I had been too close to death to not see the connection. I was supposed to be in the car that night. Had it not been for the grace of God, I might have been shot down too. The things we speak, what we name ourselves; we have to live under. I began wonder if I was serving a sentence.

None of the artists from the label came to Vegas to show their respects. And the ones that were there swiftly returned Cali. I think Tupac's death scared the shit out of everybody. Suge and I stayed in Vegas for about a week longer. During that time, I only saw him once or twice. When I did see him, all we could do is cry and talk about Pac. We were left with so many questions. We didn't know how we could move on, or if we'd ever recover. Serving time on Death Row was getting harder with Pac gone. It seemed like we were falling apart.

When we left Vegas, we went back to LA for a while. After Pac was killed, people were bolder. Death Row was no longer untouchable. We started getting threats, so Suge moved me to Michel'le's old place in Calabasas. Not long after the move, Suge had us fly to Compass Point, Bahamas to wrap up the "Christmas on Death Row" album. We were trying to get things back moving in the right direction, but it seemed like everything was working against us.

Being in Bahamas provided only a brief distraction from the hurt, heartache, and agony that was still lingering. Back in the states, they were investigating Suge for allegedly stomping the guy that he was in an altercation with at the hotel. They never questioned Orlando Anderson about his whereabouts during the shooting. They overlooked all of that and did everything that they could to prosecute Suge. To me, it didn't seem like they had any validity, but they definitely made their case.

While we were in the Bahamas, I woke up one day and realized that I couldn't get up. I couldn't get out of the bed. For weeks I was seeing a back specialist there.

After about a month in the Bahamas, I was still experiencing back pains, I was being pushed around in a wheelchair. I had to have people help me get in and out of the shower. I was almost helpless. The pain was becoming unbearable. Suge came into the studio one day and saw me lying down in the booth recording "The Christmas Song." He immediately told everyone to take the rest of the night off. Suge, his barber, Reggie Lamb, and I went back to the house that Suge was renting while we were there.

Suge's house was on the ocean. Hoping that the salt water would heal my back, we went out for a soak. There were these large rocks in the water that protected us from the sharks that swam on the other side. We drank liquor until everyone was pissy drunk. And then we prayed. We prayed to God all night long. There was a Muslim guy there who even prayed to God in Arabic. Suge had a lot of things facing him. That night in the water was the last time we talked liked that.

The next day, Suge came by the studio and gave me his Death Row chain, which was worth more than everyone's chains together. He took it off, put it around my neck, and told me to hold it down. When he left the studio, I thought he was going to the Villa, but about an hour later, Kevin Lewis called a meeting.

He asked me to pray before he began to talk. Kevin told us that Suge was on his way back to LA to turn himself in. There had been a warrant issued for his arrest. They made sure that he was gone and on the plane before they told me, because Suge didn't want me to know what was going on. We stayed at Compass Point for another week.

Suge was all over the news. Early one morning, the police came into the studio and told us that we had to leave. They escorted us to the van without giving us a chance to go back and retrieve our belongings. They wanted us to go directly from the studio to the airport. And that's what we did. We left behind our clothes, shoes and personal items. All we knew was that they no longer wanted us there. I was still having problems moving, and was still in a wheelchair. Reggie Lamb had to push me around everywhere.

We flew into Miami, but were stranded there because there had just been a hurricane. We had to sleep in the airport that night. My back pain was so bad that I cried all night long.

As soon as we got back to LA, I went to the hospital. I had no feeling in my legs; I was basically paralyzed. I couldn't get out the bed. I needed help using the bathroom and doing the things I was used to doing on my own. I had been in the hospital for two months, and hadn't heard anything from Suge.

I was in therapy, working to get better before my birthday arrived. I would tell the doctor that I was okay even though I was still in pain. It was weird not to hear from Suge, because we normally talked every day. He was in prison, but it was not like him to cease all communication. At the least, he would send a message through someone else. But there were no messages, no notes, and no phone calls. I knew that he had been in communication with someone, but I couldn't understand why he wouldn't talk to me. When he gave me his chain, it felt like a father-son moment. But at this point, I didn't know what to think. His people were telling me that he couldn't have visitors and that he had no phone calls. I believed them; I was naïve.

When I was discharged from the hospital on October 30, I still hoped that Suge would find a way to talk to me. Even though I hadn't talked to Suge, I was still thinking about how the police had hemmed him up. I didn't understand why they would go to so much trouble to lock him up for allegedly stomping on some guy when Tupac's killer was free. I'd seen a lot of movies and they led me to believe that when people were involved in an altercation, and

154

later one of them is hurt or dies, they investigate all parties involved. Orlando Anderson would have been number one on my list. They went all around that point and arrested Suge for the fight, but never arrested anyone for the murder of Tupac.

I think the authorities had it out for Suge. He could be a pain in the ass. The fact that he had millions behind him only further exacerbated things. This was the beginning of niggas having money outside of sports. It was new, and I think it made them nervous. Suge had money, and he had power. And they wanted him off the streets. They were more focused on taking him down than solving Pac's murder. It was a tough time for me. Our chain was broken; I had lost both Tupac and Suge.

Chapter 20: Stranded on Death Row

The Christmas album was slated to be released a month or so after I was discharged from the hospital. We finished all of the songs, and made the release date. With Suge locked up, I knew that things were going to change, but I didn't know that they would change the way that did.

Before Suge went to jail, he always made sure that I had plenty of money to do holiday shopping for my family. He always made sure that I was good when I went home to Chicago for Christmas. This year was vastly different. It was the beginning of Death Row Records' demise. Tupac was gone, Suge was locked up, Snoop had left the label, and all of the other artists seemed to be doing their own thing.

The studio was beginning to feel like a desert. I was still there everyday recording and hanging out because the studio was my element. I would be there at least fifteen hours out of the day. With the transitions, it gradually began more difficult for me to gain access to the studio. I went from people calling me Mr. Knight, to being treated like a stepchild. The people who took over had no respect for the previous structure. They were on their own stuff, and I was left to figure things out for myself.

One morning I woke up to go to one of Suge's court dates. When I got there, Norris, Suge's brother-in-law said to me, "I need that chain before you leave today." I cursed his ass out and kept it moving. Suge had left the chain in my possession. I felt responsible for it. I didn't want to betray his trust by just handing it over. I was trying my best to be the man he had taught me to be. But Norris didn't give up; he called me just about every day. The next time I saw him in court, I gave him the chain.

When court was over, Suge turned around and nodded his head as the sheriffs escorted him out. After attending a few more court sessions, we found out that Suge would not be given a bond. He had a long list of charges brought against him.

The judge said that the fight in Vegas was a violation of his probation, and that he would be looking at seven to eight years. When I heard this, I sat in the back of the court and cried like a baby. When the people back at the office found out about this, things went from bad to worse.

They started giving me my $2K monthly salary late. I was supposed to be paid on the first of the month, but they would pay me in the middle of the month if at all.

Michel'le was handling Suge's business. Before Suge went to jail, we were cool, but once he was locked up, she turned into a different person. In fact, I wouldn't be surprised if she was the reason Snoop left. She started cutting off our checks and not returning phone calls—just doing mean shit. She was getting paid $100K a month to run things, but I guess that wasn't enough for her. It was like she was trying to bring Death Row down. And I'm not sure if Suge had any idea what was happening. Her actions were extreme. She'd sign checks upside down so the bank wouldn't cash them. When I finally got through to her people, they told me that Michel'le wanted to know if I had saved any money. She cared nothing about Suge's guardianship, or my contract, which entitled me to a minimum of $2K per month.

After my car caught a blowout, they started playing games about giving it back to me. To make matters worse, our utilities were turned off because I couldn't pay the bill. When I called the office to tell them about my situation, they told me that they would get around to it. I knew not to hold my breath. I had no car, no lights, and the Feds were coming to my house with questions about Suge. We got our things together and went back to Chicago for the holidays.

When I arrived in Chicago, I had gifts, but not as many as I usually had. I had the little money Trina had helped me save, but I couldn't party like I usually did when I came home.

I was in Chicago for about two weeks when I called my house in LA to check the voicemail. When dialed the number, a girl answered the phone, so I hung up immediately because I thought I had dialed the wrong number. I picked up the phone and called again. This time, she said hello with an attitude. "I'm trying to call my voice mail and I keep getting you," I said.

The voice on the other line was Stormy, Suge's baby mama. She had moved into my house. "The office didn't tell you?" she asked. I immediately hung up from her and called the office, but I couldn't reach anyone because the office was closed for the holidays. I ended up getting in contact with Suge's assistant. As soon as he answered the phone, I went off.

Roy had no idea what I was talking about. "Let me try to get Norris on the phone. I'll call you back," he said. But I didn't hear back from anybody until I was on my way back home around the first of the year. With Trina and Ashley back home in Chicago, I went back to LA to try to sort things out. As soon as I got there, I went to the office. I stayed there all day, into the evening. I ended up staying at my homie Young Buck's spot for a few weeks.

When I went to Suge's shop to check on my car, I saw that it was in the work stall. When I tried to get it, they gave me the runaround about it. I never saw my car again after that day. I couldn't get through to Suge, and the people in the office were treating me like shit. I went off on them so much that they started sending me to voicemail.

After many months of living with other people, being denied my car, and housing, I started to believe that Suge was mad at me. But I hadn't done anything to warrant his silence. Whenever anyone had any words about him, I always defended him. He had taken care of me. Even when I was broke and hungry, I remained loyal. We were so close that a lot of people had a problem with it. As his son, I had a front row seat to everything. Now that they had some power, they did everything they could to keep me away from him. I knew that someone had said something that was off.

When I would see Michel'le, she would be so rude to me for no reason. When she was on the bottle, and drunk, I used to help Suge get her out of the car and into the bed, but I guess those times didn't matter. She was a woman in power and she didn't care who she ran over to maintain it.

I didn't know what move I was going to make. My grandmother was worried. She would tell me to come back home. With my money getting low, and the pressure of everything else weighing heavy on me, I did just that.

Going back to the Chi was one of the most difficult decisions I had to make. As soon as I got there, everybody wanted to know what was going on. They wanted to know why I wasn't in Cali anymore. I wasn't partying at all. I was trying to save every piece of change I had.

I would spend some time talking to Pac's mother, Afeni, and she would tell me that things would get better. She said that she was having some challenges getting Pac's estate in order. K-Ci, JoJo, and Darius were some of the few people who treated me the same. Darius even fed me on a few occasions; he was still family. But Ray J and some of my other Hollywood friends stopped answering my calls. Moments like this were the very reason we formed Kommittee. Now, he was acting as if he didn't know me. After I left LA, I heard that he was going around telling people that I was in Chicago, strung out on drugs. That couldn't have been further from the truth. You really find out who's got your back when you really need them. When Death Row was on top, everybody was my friend. Ray J wasn't even old enough to drive yet. I would talk to his mom and she would let him ride out with us.

We partied, traveled, and supported each other's careers. But when I moved back to Chicago, Ray J kicked me out the group and changed the name to "Knock Out." As tight as we were, no one had my back when I was down and out.

At one point I couldn't get family away from me, but when things got bad everybody kept their distance. I guess they were scared that I was going to need some help. All of the people that I had helped when I had money were nowhere to be found. Some of my "friends" went from laughing with me, to laughing at me.

Once I finally talked to Suge on the phone, he said, "Danny Boy you grown now. You should know what to do." Clearly, I didn't because nothing got better. I was still at home in Chicago on the verge of having nothing. My bank account was running low and I was sleeping on couches all over the city. I knew that I was wearing out my welcome at some of those places.

All of the things that I was used to were no more. The money, friends, and the good times were all gone. I was slowly falling apart at the seams. To make matters worse, the love of my life was falling out of love with me. For a minute,

I felt like giving everything up, but I did everything I could to keep moving forward.

Trina and I fought and argued every day. She was back living with her mom; I was living in between my sister Orlean and my grandmother's house. I had been so used to Death Row providing for us, but I knew that it was over. There were a few more phone conversations with Suge, but after a while, he cut me off like a bad habit; there was no more communication.

He was in San Louis Obispo, California which was almost five hours away from LA. I was in Chicago with no money, and no idea of how to get to him. I started going to family members to get them to sponsor my trip.

I had been so tired of dealing with the people that Suge had left in charge. Norris was out. Reggie Wright, the owner of Wright Way Security and Michel'le became the executives of the company. Reggie and Michel'le played off each other so well. He was just as dirty as she had become. I couldn't get any money out of them. When I was old enough to find out about royalties and publishing is when they really changed up on me.

When I requested an accounting statement from the office, I received papers that had certain things highlighted on them:

1) Lease for car (I thought it was a gift)

2) Jewelry (Another gift I was paying for)

3) Advances (Some amounts I never knew about)

4) Money Suge sent for my mother's funeral (Who charges someone for bereavement gifts?)

After number four, I knew that my loyalty for Death Row was over. Obviously I wasn't dealing with people of compassion, empathy or morals. I couldn't get anything out of them. I knew that Suge didn't know about everything that they were doing at the office, but he did know that they weren't giving me anything. And he knew that I was hungry and had no place to stay.

When I found out where they were holding Suge, I started writing him letters. I filled up an entire notepad and sent it to him. In my initial letters, I asked him how he was holding up behind bars. I never wanted to pressure him on paper about what I was going through. I received letters from him, but they never really answered any questions about what to do, or how he would help me out of my situation. This dude had adopted me and was supposed to be my dad, but now he had left me stranded.

Suge gave me the runaround, but I remained loyal to him. I wrote him a letter expressing how bad I wanted my project to come out, and how much I needed to be on stage and share my gift. Most importantly, I wanted to be able to provide for my daughter, Ashley. In the letter, I expressed to him that I thought that it was like old times, and that I could talk to him about anything, just like a son could do his father. I asked him to release my song, and put the album out.

I told Suge that I felt like a bird that sings and is locked in a jar that no one could hear, and if the bird master would just open the top to the jar, the world would be able to hear the bird sing. After that letter, he finally called me and asked me if I could come up to see him. He told me that he had me on the list to be able to come and visit, and told me to fill out the paperwork that he had sent me.

I filled out the paperwork, and sent it in. Some weeks later, I got a letter back saying that my paperwork had been denied due to felonies on my record: *"Transportation of a dangerous substance, auto theft and unlawful use of a weapon."* Something was wrong because I was afraid to even get a traffic ticket. I was advised to take my fingerprints and go to the police department to get a background check. When my rap sheet came back, I had the same charges that I was informed about when I filled out the paperwork.

The crimes that I had supposedly committed were in four different states. When I went to the sheriff's office, I gave them my fingerprints and other information; they sent me to the magistrate to have the charges removed.

The last department I went to was in Crown Point, Indiana. I got there to the station and they said that I had an outstanding warrant for my arrest. I turned myself in, and they compared my weight and picture this time. When I saw the picture, I realized that it was my nephew, Andre. It hurt like hell because he knew that I was trying to make something out of myself. When I went to court that day, the judge dismissed the case and gave clearance for the charges to be removed.

I called my grandmother crying. How could family do this to one another? If you were going to commit a crime, don't use my name! Use a name from a song, or a movie or something if you can't own up to your actions. Don't use my shit!

I was happy to have handled that situation. It was going to take some months before I could even reapply to go and visit Suge. When I did apply, it took only thirty days before I was approved. I quickly came up with a plan to go out and see Suge.

With the help of family and friends, we raised about a thousand dollars, but we needed about three thousand more for food and lodging. My god brother, Obie introduced me to his guy named D. When D found out what I was trying to do, he gave me his brand new, top of the line conversion van, and about two thousand dollars in cash.

A week later, my new team and I made the drive from Chicago to California. After making the five-hour drive to the prison, I was finally able to see Suge. We walked around the track for a while. I could tell that he wanted to say something, but I he was trying to protect my feelings. I knew Suge, so I asked him, "For real. Be real with me. How come you just stopped talking to me? Why did you cut me off?" He tried to beat around the bush, but then he finally broke down. "Danny Boy, I been in here all this time, and you never tried to come see or write me. They told me that you said, fuck me and Death Row," he said. I didn't know what to say to him, because he knew better. "You believe that?" I asked him. He knew that I was loyal, but I guess this was just the beginning of him loosing who he was.

Reggie Wright, and all of the others that were stealing and trying to live like Suge while he was locked up were there too. When we got back to where they were, I went off on all of them about the shit they had been talking. They were mad as hell by the end of that visit. Suge asked me to come back in two weeks, which meant we had to stay in Cali much longer than planned. The money began running low, but we weren't leaving. I was hoping that our visits would bring about a change.

Doug, my security, had left me for Public Announcement, and a week later, my cousin, whom I had never gotten into it with before were arguing so bad that I called her a bitch. She hopped on the plane the next morning and left us there. That left Craig, Marcus and I. We had very little money, and after a two-month stay in California, we headed back home. When we pulled up on the South Side of Chicago, we had eight dollars left. Marcus and Craig got something to drink, and I got a cigar and a five-dollar bag.

After all the time I had spent back in Cali, Suge still didn't seem to know what was going on in *his* company. I knew that it was time for me to let go of the past. I would have to make it work on my own.

Chapter 21: Letting Go of the Past

Being back home showed me that some people still cared. When promoters found out that I was in Chicago, they reached out and were ready to book me. I also did some studio work with artists like Do or Die and Twista as I worked my way back into the Chicago music scene. All of the money I was making at this time was either owed to a bill or to someone that I had borrowed from.

As much as I was struggling, people were still recognizing me. In a way, I was still a celebrity to them. I remember times that I would be in a fast food restaurant and people would recognize who I was and would go out of the restaurant to grab more people to come meet me. I enjoyed moments like this, it was something to see how many people's lives were touched through Tupac's music, and I was grateful to have been a part of that.

Everywhere I went, there were people who knew me. Often, they wanted to talk to me about what it was like to be on Death Row. They would always ask me if I was afraid of Suge. If I had a dime for every time I was asked that question...

It seemed like I just couldn't get up on my feet. It was a dark time for me. I was losing everything. And felt like the people who could help, had turned their backs on me. It was hard for me to trust people. If it weren't for my grandmother, I would have taken my own life. I felt just that low. I never thought that I would come to that point. But my grandmother kept praying for me. And she always knew what to say.

I had to shake off the depression. I had a child to provide for, so I did what I could to find work. I did a couple of appearances at local High Schools. Those times were a great boost for my ego. It was hard to move through the crowds. The kids were chasing me down the halls on some Michael Jackson shit. It was crazy! When the promoters saw the crowd's reactions, they ended up putting me on a high school tour. This is when I hired a manager by the name of Dee Daniels. It was so hard to hire another manager/publicist because at this point, I didn't trust anybody in the industry.

I had already been fucked over by the best: Suge Knight, Reggie "Pork Butt" Wright, Michel'le, and the rest of the office goons. I started booking radio interviews, and promoters were paying me $2,000-$3,000 per show. It felt like things were looking up. Dee Daniels hooked up a feature with jazz saxophonist, Danny Learman to record the vocals on a song called "Take My Breath Away." The song played on the radio for over two years. It was a good move for me. That song got me a ton of jobs as a wedding singer. It really provided me with the opportunity to get out and show people that I wanted it. I just didn't realize how many people were interested in what I had to offer. I had been so busy trying to get Death Row to act right, that I had forgotten who I was.

I had been depending on my resource instead on the source, which was God. During my time in Chicago, I experienced something that I just wasn't used to. Music was healing. It became my therapy.

I appreciated every moment I spent back home. I had a chance to be around family and friends. There, I formed a new team (Linda Reese, Billy, Craig, Tim, and Red) who helped keep me focused. I was back to where I had started, back to my roots. I would sing at the funerals, birthday parties, graduations, it didn't matter. I sang wherever people wanted me to sing because it was helping me eat. During this time in my life, I met a lot of great people, and built a lot of great relationships. It was my humbling season. And I was grateful for it.

We've all seen or heard stories about musicians and singers losing their minds after situations and circumstances occurred. I wasn't going to let my story end like that. I did whatever I could to stay motivated. I would listen to old school music all the time. It would pump me up, and lift my spirits. When I heard Bobby Womack sing "Nobody Wants You (When You're Down and Out)," it was like the song was the soundtrack of my life at the moment. It expressed my feelings, and how some people treated me. My process was painful, but in the end, I was shown what true friendship and love was about.

*****

Soon the shows slowed down, and the promoters knew me no more. I was still singing at local funeral homes every chance I got. One day I got a call from a funeral director who said to me, "Why didn't you tell me you sang for Suge Knight and Snoop Dogg, and all those guys?" Before I could even say anything, he told me that he had a service for a young man that had been murdered. I had one hour to get up to the funeral home. I got dressed and went right over. They had purchased every CD I had sung on—

even my singles. They used them to show the family who I was.

Sometimes it was overwhelming, at other times, it was a blessing. After the service, I went back to talk to the embalmer. He was a friend of mine named Lemont. I walked into the prep room and asked him if I could work with him. He was preparing to dress a body, and I was trying not to look scared, but I *was*. I was still interested in working there though. Lemont told me to come back the next morning.

When I left out of the funeral home, the first thing I did was go to the store and buy a uniform. By the time I got to the house, I was looking like Dr. Steward. I couldn't wait for the next morning.

I was up really early in the morning eating my bacon sandwich, and ironing my gear. I was ready to hit the door. I made it to A.R. Leak Funeral Home before anyone else did.

I sat around and waited until Lemont was ready to begin working. After about thirty minutes, we entered the prep room. I was so scared but I couldn't wait to see what was about to happen. I had been interested in Mortuary Science since I was a little boy.

Lemont opened the door and turned on the lights. There were six bodies lying on the table. Some of them had just come in, and the others were ready to be transferred to the casket. I didn't know what to do because when I walked, there was no clear path that I could take without brushing up against a table that had a dead body on it.

Lemont told me to get one of the lab jackets off the hook and put it on. The only problem was that the jacket was on the other side of the table near another dead body. I had to walk to the other side and get the jacket without letting him know that I was about to shit on myself. Man…you talking about the craziest feeling ever! I was more than afraid!

After I put on my jacket, I watched Lemont take some stuff out of a plastic bag. He turned to me, and began to explain that the person that we were preparing to work on had been posted. This meant that the Coroner had performed an autopsy on them. He placed these bags at the feet of the deceased. As I looked on, my stomach felt like it was turning inside out. I wished that I would have worn a pamper that day.

Before I knew it, Lemont was standing over the body. He pulled the man's hairline from the back of his neck to the front. It was inside out. He removed the cranium, and took the brain out of the bag. He handed it to me. "Put it back in" he said to me. I can't even express what it felt like to hold someone's brain in my hands. It was some "Tales from the Crypt" type shit.

When he opened the man's chest, I was curious to see what it looked like inside. I leaned over peered in. That messed me up! I couldn't eat ribs for a year after that. It was the nastiest thing I had ever seen, and Lemont was standing there doing his job like it was nothing.

After I had worked with Lemont on the first case, I dreamed about it for a week. I couldn't go back. I lied to Lemont and told him that I had to go out of town. After a short time, I was ready to go back in the prep room and try it again.

I didn't think that it could get any scarier than the first time. It didn't. The next case brought about different emotions. This time, we would be working on a little boy that I had just seen on the news the night before who had died of meningitis. As I stood there and looked at this child, my eyes began to fill up with tears. I was crying like he was kin to me.

Before we could work on him, we had to study and get instruction on how to care for the body. Meningitis is an airborne disease, and we had to treat it carefully. After reading and talking with the Master of Mortuary Science, we were finally ready to proceed.

We covered our entire bodies, and went inside the room. Once in the room, Lemont handed me a bottle of

Clorox bleach. He told me to open it, and pour it all over the little boy's body. My eyes were burning and tearing up because I couldn't believe what I was doing to this baby, but I had to follow safety protocol.

Lemont told me to make sure I poured the bleach in the boy's eyes, mouth, and anywhere there was an opening. I began to pour bleach in the little boys mouth, and the tears that were building up began to roll down my face.

I felt so bad, because of what this baby had to endure. I began to think about my daughter and my nieces and nephews. I couldn't imagine what his family was going through. He looked as if he was asleep.

When the mother came in to give us the little boy's clothes, she was distraught. All she had was his school uniform. Before she could hand us the bag, I offered to buy him some clothes. I went to the store and purchased a shirt, tie, and slacks. I felt like I was shopping for someone I knew, at least you would have thought so the way I was crying.

When the owner of the store found out what I was doing, he practically gave me the clothes. When I got back to the funeral home that day, I helped dress him. It was quite emotional. Back in LA, we were rocking Death Row chains, thinking we were invincible, but death was real. I had a front row seat, and it was sobering.

Working at AR Leak really humbled me. During the times that I felt like I didn't want to go on, I would go in to work and see someone whose life had been taken away from them. Just to see how the families would react to the death of their loved one made me realize that I would never wish that type of hurt on anyone; I had everything to live for.

Chapter 22: Tug of War

My work at the funeral home brought in some income, but it wasn't nearly enough. As time went on, I took on additional jobs. I would sing at funerals during the day, and clean offices at night. Even with two jobs, I still struggled to make ends meet. I was living with Trina and her mother, Linda. Trina and I weren't getting along at all. She slept in the room, and I slept on the couch. I was still very much in love with her, but she had moved on. She had begun to date, which made things awkward for everyone.

After trying unsuccessfully to win back Trina's affection, I finally decided to move on. That's when I started dating Keke. I had known Keke since grammar school. I'd had the biggest crush on her back in the day, but she was out of my league. Before I went to LA, she wouldn't give me any play, but now that I had a little bit of celebrity, she opened up to my advances. Once we started dating, we had a hard time being apart.

Living with Trina made it difficult for Keke and me to grow in our relationship. Truth is, I was still torn. But Trina was over me and desperately wanted me out of her mother's home. I knew that it was time for me to do something; we were arguing constantly. And I was hurt and full of rage. I was moving on because she gave me no choice; she had made a conscious decision to date other people. My jealousy was pushing me over the edge. It got to the point that whenever she would leave, I would check her underwear to see if she had been doing something with the guys she was dating. It was some lame shit. It was time for me to go. I took a job as a Family Counselor at Oak Ridge Cemetery. It was the cemetery my mother was buried at. During my lunch hour, I would sit at my mother's gravesite and eat. I eventually found myself there on my off days as well.

During this time, my grandmother's health began to fail. I would visit my mother's gravesite at lunch, then after work, I would visit my grandmother at Rush Presbyterian hospital. My grandmother was my rock. Now, I was sitting at her bedside, praying for her to get better.

Me and my cousin, Kimberla would sometimes sit with her—talking and singing. Soon everyone was coming to visit her. We could tell that her health was declining. One day, she began to call the names of all of her children that had preceded her in death. When she got to my mother's name, she said "Dorothy, catch the wheel. Don't let that wheel fall." It was chilling. I didn't understand what she was saying, and I wondered if it was a sign. I thought that if the wheel fell, she would die, because she was so adamant about it not falling.

Chapter 23: Missing the Matriarch

The last time I had saw my grandmother, we were singing hymns. When we were done singing, she said, "Tell Dion to leave that washer machine alone." Then she started calling Michael, but neither he nor my cousin Dion were around. I thought she was becoming senile. If I would've have known that she was about to make her transition, I would have never left her side. But God always had a way of protecting me. It was not meant for me to be there. I would have been a wreck. No matter how frequent death came, it was always difficult. I don't think I could have taken it.

They next day, me and my friend, Craig were on our way to the hospital from the South Side. We made a stop on Kedzie Street to grab something to eat from the Burger King. I was joking around and bothering all of the workers like usual. They were laughing so hard; we were having a good time. While I was placing my order, my phone rang. When I answered, all I could hear was crying in the background. It was Kimberla. My grandmother was gone.

I yelled out and began crying. Craig and I jumped in the Jeep and headed to the hospital. We ran lights all the way there. When we exited the elevator, I could hear the cries of my family members. They were yelling in heartbreaking agony.

My grandmother looked as if she was just sleeping. I sat on the floor next to her bed and held her hand. She was so cold, and stiff. It was a stillness I knew all too well. I couldn't take it. It was like losing a mother all over again. I held her hand so tight. I was so afraid of facing life's challenges without her. Elsie Stamps, the backbone of our family, was gone.

Family flew in from everywhere as we were finalizing the funeral arrangements. I was going back and forth to the funeral home helping out in whatever capacity I could. My aunt and I dressed her, and fixed her hair. It was a difficult time, but I had to make sure that she looked her best.

On the day of my grandmother's service, Trina's mom and I rented two luxury Town Cars. We all rode to the service together. Just as had been the case with my mother's funeral, people showed up in droves for my grandmother. Cars were double-parked as far as I could see. And just as I had at my mother's funeral, I struggled to sing my final tribute. After the service, my grandmother was buried next to my grandfather, Lymon Stamps Sr. It was a strange reality that brought me to my knees.

Chapter 24: Emotionally Bankrupt

Suge had been in jail for about a year before I realized that I would never be able to take control of my career as long as I was attached to Death Row. Between the pitiful accountings, and Michel'le's meddling, I was done. Pac's record sales went through the roof after he was killed, but I never received any royalties. Afeni had told me that we would be all right, but it seemed that she had forgotten about me. With no other option, I had to issue a cease and desist against the estate. Nothing like this would have ever happened if Tupac were still alive. He was my brother; he would have made sure that I was taken care of.

After the cease and desist, Afeni's lawyers came up with a minimum royalty for "I Ain't Mad at Cha" and "Toss It Up." For whatever reason, they didn't calculate for the other records I recorded with Pac. When I tried to collect, they said that the check had been cut and sent to Suge. At this point, it was about much more than money. I didn't need to get rich; I just wanted things to be right, to be fair. Other people were making money off of me, I wasn't being paid any royalties, and there was no one to look out for my best interests, so I had to do it for myself.

The prospect of taking on a label like Death Row would be costly, but I hoped that I could assemble a team who could make that happen. I ran into Shorty Capone during this time, but he was unapologetic. Guys like Shorty don't apologize for anything. He was a crook. But his partner, Chili, was a good guy. He looked out for me, and made sure I ate. He eventually convinced Shorty to help me. After all we had been through, Shorty came up with a thousand dollars to help with my case.

A thousand dollars wouldn't do much. I needed to make some money if I was going to get off of Death Row.

Despite the fact that I had been away from LA for a while, I still kept in contact with Queen, Death Row's secretary. Queen knew the legendary Teena Marie. She ended up getting me an audition. When I sang for her, she said, "Nigga, you can sing!" I was happy to book the gig. Teena was cool. I ended up doing about six shows with her. She wanted me to sing Rick James' part on "Fire and Desire." While we were rehearsing the song, Rick James actually showed up. I was out there singing when I heard him scream "Bitch! Who in there singing my song?" Man, it was a good time. Rick liked my singing, and Teena was hyped! When they died, they took something special with them.

My connection to Death Row put me in the presence of so many greats who are no longer here. There was Whitney Houston, who would always ask me to sing when she saw me. And Left Eye, with whom I had recorded with before she died. I had known Aaliyah, Heavy D, and Roger Troutman; eventually they'd all leave this earth. As much as I enjoyed those opportunities, I was tired of losing people; I was tired of being on Death Row. It was time for me to get off!

I contacted many attorneys, but none of them were interested in taking on Death Row. I wasn't getting anywhere. It wasn't until I got in contact with Clive Davis, that things began to work in my favor. Clive had a son who was an attorney. When Trina's mother and I drove up to New York to meet with him, he advised me to file for bankruptcy. By filing for Chapter 7, I would be cleared of all my debts and financial obligations. I filled for bankruptcy, and the case was discharged. I was finally off of Death Row.

Chapter 25: That's My DJ

After dating for a while, we learned that Keke was pregnant, so we decided it was time to move in together. She had been talking to her hair stylist, Ms. Joann, about our apartment search. She had a place that was close to where we had grown up. We went by to see the apartment, but we didn't have the money to pay the security deposit. When I saw that the place needed a little work, I asked Ms. Joann if I could complete the needed repairs in lieu of the security deposit. She gave us the keys that day.

We painted, tore out the bathroom floor, and put up a shower door. When we finished, Ms. Joan was happy. She was glad to have us as tenants. We moved into the apartment just before Danny Boy Steward Jr. was born.

Danny Jr. was born on October 2, 2002, twenty-nine days before my birthday. What a gift!

With a baby and a new apartment, I needed more money. I found a job working security. I had met the supervisor of the company at an event that I had sung for. I gave him a call, and went in for the interview. The interview was untraditional, to say the least. We mostly talked about Death Row, Tupac, and my journey through the industry. By the time I left that office, I had my uniform and ID badge in hand. I was still working the cemetery during the day and security at night.

On my first day going to work as officer Steward, I was cleaner than the board of health! That day I had taken my pants to be tailored, I had on some GBX shoes that were all shined up, and a turtleneck underneath my uniform. It didn't matter what job I had, I was always clean and my pants were always tailored.

I was stationed at the railroad, and I had permission to lock people up if they were trespassing. I don't know why they told me that, because I was locking people up at least twice a week. You know u can't give a nigga that much juice that quick. While I worked my security job, I was trying my best to continue working at the cemetery. But juggling the two proved to be too much. Since I was having such a good time being a fake officer, I decided to let the cemetery job go.

Things on the job were going good, but in the home front, Keke and I stayed at each other's throats. We would've been the perfect couple if she didn't have it out for my daughter. Ashley was just a kid, but Keke was jealous. She was jealous of Ashley and of the relationship that I had with Trina and her mother. Trina and I were mature in the way we parented. And her mother would always be a mother to me. We were family, and we later became the best of friends. But that was the extent of the relationship. The romance was a thing of the past, but Keke couldn't deal with that. She thought that I was giving all my money to Trina and Ashley.

When Christmas came around, things only got worse. Keke went shopping, but never got anything for my Ashley. And it wasn't because we didn't have the money. Our landlord had told us to keep our December rent as a gift. In addition, my manager and good friend, Dee Daniels had given me money for the kids. When I learned that Keke had neglected to buy Ashley any gifts, I just gave all of the money to Trina for Ashley.

When Keke found out, she said, "You always giving them bitches something."

"Who you calling a bitch?" I said.

"Trina's a bitch, yo fake mama's a bitch, and Ashley is a bitch!" she said.

When Ashley's name left her mouth, I snatched her ass up so quickly. This wasn't an easy task, because she liked to fight. She *had* to be ready to fight to make a statement as fucked up as the one she made to me about my daughter. It was wrong of me to put my hands on a woman, but I was immature back then. That's something I'd never encourage. I should've just walked away. I just couldn't believe that she could fix her mouth to call my baby a bitch. We were yelling and fighting when she tried to call the police on me. I pulled every phone out of the socket and left the apartment to go

cool off.

Chapter 26: Club Paje'

When I went to work the next day, I was already in a bad mood. After the argument, I had stayed out until the next morning. That day I had to work a double shift. I got to work as usual, but by the middle of the night, I was tired. I got out of the car and walked the railroads and the yards.

At break time, I got back in the car. I had almost made it the whole night, but two hours before my shift ended, I fell asleep. If my old supervisor were still there, things would have gone differently. But I had a new supervisor, and he was an asshole. When he tapped on my window, I let it down, and told him that I wasn't asleep. We argued for ten minutes before I rolled the window back up on him. Like the asshole he was, he stayed there until my shift ended. As I was clocking out, he told me that he was writing me up. What did he tell me that for? I went off on him, and left. I had the nerve to show up for work the next day and they didn't say anything.

I was off that Thursday, so I went up to Club Pajé. Pajé was a famous bar and restaurant where the "Who's Who" of Chicago hung out. The club was owned by a fellow named Rock. Rock treated me like I was his nephew; I'd known him since I was fourteen.

The place was crowded and business was booming. I told Rock that I wanted a second job. I wasn't playing either. He told me that I could come whenever I wanted to. I was back, and ready to work, in less than two weeks.

My first day at Pajé, I showed up dressed in my all black, ready to service tables. When I arrived, Rock's sister-in-law, who was the server/bartender/manager, told me that I was going to work with this very flamboyant guy. I told her that I wasn't working with him. He was too flashy for me. He was calling straight men, boo. And he was loud! She let me work with someone else that night.

I made all of $12 that night, and I still had to tip the bus boy out of that. I had watched the flamboyant guy rack in the dough. The next night, I wanted to work with him. One thing about him was that he knew how to make that money. He knew how to work the room.

He had to serve a party of nearly thirty people, so we worked it together. When they arrived, and he began seating them, I noticed that it was Lil' Kim and her crew. When I saw her, I fell back because I didn't want her to see me or notice me. Kim and I had never really moved in the same circles, but she knew who I was.

I stayed working the opposite end of the table. They were ordering food, drinks, and Champagne all night. When the bill came, it was over $4K. When there were over seven people in the party, we automatically received a percentage of the total amount. It was shaping up to be a good night for me.

When he gave them the bill, they paid and were getting ready to leave when Lil' Kim walked up to me and said, "Danny Boy you have an incredible voice. You *gone* be okay!" She grabbed my hand and put something in it. I could tell it was money. I put it in my pocket and thanked her. When they left, I went into the bathroom to see how much it was. It was almost eight hundred dollars. I shouted right there in the bathroom! God knew that I needed that money. I had bills at the house that needed to be paid, and God had sent an angel in the likes of Lil' Kim to bless me. I am forever grateful for her kind gesture.

Not only did we get what we needed for bills, but I was given an overflow blessing. I had more than enough to do what needed to be done. When I got home, I couldn't wait to go to work the next night. But the next few nights were slow. In three days, I had only made a little over a hundred dollars.

One night I was working and a patron noticed me and said, "Damn. Suge whooped yo ass and now he got you serving tables?" That was the night I learned how to make drinks with a twist, you know, Coke, with a little twist of dishwater mix. Or instead of finger foods, you give them finger drinks with a specialty-spit-shine. It was a joy to watch his old disrespectful ass guzzle it down. I kept that nigga with refills all night. After that night, I had made up in my mind that I would no longer be ashamed to service tables.

When I got back on the clock, I used who I was to my advantage. I was singing for people's birthdays, and I was serving just about every Chicago Bull and Chicago Bear. I was getting my money. It was nothing for me to take home five to six hundred dollars every three to four days. Jamal Crawford used to hit me hard. He would order a five-dollar drink and still tip me a hundred dollars.

My finances were improving, but Keke and I were getting into it over every little thing. Her jealousy was out of control. I came home from a long shift to find the door locked and most of my things sitting out in the hallway.

I got on the phone, and called my cousin, Kimberla. She came all the way from the South Side of Chicago in the middle of the night to rescue me from Keke and her chaos. It was the third time she had done this. And I was out! I got the rest of my things and moved in with Kimberla. I just couldn't get this relationship thing right. Once again, I was a baby daddy.

Living with Kimberla was a big relief for me because she and I got along so well. If there was something that she or I did that one of us didn't like, we let it be known up front. The other thing about it was that we knew each other so well that if we were getting on each other's nerves, we gave each other space.

Staying with Kim, I was able to focus on my music. It was the first time I had lived with someone that wasn't my girlfriend. The best part of this move was that I no longer had anyone to answer to. Kimberla was my cousin; together we could make things happen.

Chapter 27: Subpoenaed to Tha Row

I lived with my cousin Kimberla for about a year. During this time, we ran into many wanna-be investors who either didn't have the money, or tried to take advantage of us. I was doing plays, recorded on other artist's albums, and even had a single out, but I was ready for the real thing. With no concrete investors, I was ready to give up. Then Suge was released from jail.

Suge was out for about a week before he called. "What you got up?" he asked. I was working a regular job. There was not much to tell. Suge asked me if I wanted to come back to LA. Three weeks later, I was on my way back to LA. We were finally going to make this music thing happen. My people thought it was a bad idea, but I didn't listen. I just wanted it so bad that I had to take the chance. When I arrived in LA, I went up to the office and waited around for Suge. When he got there, we went to get something to eat. This time things were really different. There were so many new faces. I felt like an outsider. And some of the new guys treated me like I didn't belong. They were riding around in luxury cars, and wearing Death Row chains. It was like I was watching someone else play out my life. I realized how stupid I had been to ride around in cars and live in homes that didn't belong to me. It was just status, and it was short-lived.

Suge was different. He was more frugal. Instead of handing out thousands, he was handing out hundreds. But he seemed off when it came to music. It was like he was trying to recreate the old Death Row. He had even signed a Snoop Dogg look-alike, and a guy that sounded like Pac. It wasn't personal for me; I just didn't need a Tupac replacement. There was only one Pac; And a Snoop look-alike? That was some crazy shit. Suge even had a few guys who thought they could sing. None of it was working for me.

Suge had dangled the title of Assistant Producer, so I was there to make that happen, but the new music was some of the worst shit I had ever heard. They put the fake Snoop on records with real Tupac; they were destroying legendary work. Suge had a guy named Butch running the studio and mastering records. This dude had become a producer overnight. He was fucking up records!

I was working right alongside Suge, but this time I was an adult. I watched his every move, just like I know he was watching mine. I had a chance to see the new Suge. He was still a nice guy when he wasn't being childish and starting shit. He was putting together a new label called, Tha Row.

During the Death Row days, I was never nervous living in LA. I'd always felt safe. But this was a new day, and Tha Row didn't have that same level of respect. Anything that represented that establishment became a target. I had to make sure that I was strapped every time I went to the studio or office. I was not going to go back to Chicago in a casket.

Chapter 28: Party In The Closet

Everything was so accessible in Hollywood. If I wanted weed, there was always a dealer around with whatever I needed. There was really no judgement—everyone was doing the same things. Even orgies were commonplace. They were easy to set up. There were always women around waiting for someone to bag them, and wife them up. I had had my share of sex parties, so it did not come as a surprise when I was invited to a party hosted by one of my celebrity friends.

When I walked in, I was tripped out to find that there were no women; there were only men. I mean big time actors, Grammy Award winners, and even rappers all over each other like it was perfectly normal.

I had been with guys before. When we were teenagers, Ray J, me, and some of our friends would have our own little parties. We'd be smoking weed and watching porn. It would start with one of us pulling down our pants while the others pretended not to watch. Sometimes we would sleep in the bed together and, touch on each other. We'd be at Ray J's house in The Valley. Brandy would be in one room, and we would be in the next. We'd still have our girls, and I had a child at the time. It was just something we did. It wasn't like we were in a relationship, it was fun, experimentation, and perfectly normal for a group of Hollywood kids.

The shit that me and the homies did, did not compare to what I was seeing at this party. For one, we are all adults. These niggas were in the room doing some serious shit! They were going hard. I was scared as hell when I got there though because I thought that I would run into someone that knew Suge or someone from the label, but the party was turning me on. I wanted to do something, but I was afraid that it would get back to Suge. I got a little head, but it was nothing compared to what was really going on.

This is when I realized that I might be bisexual. Hell, who in Hollywood wasn't? Most of the niggas that I knew were. Every party that I went to, I found out about another male entertainer that was a part of the lifestyle.

My next experience was with one of my boys that was a part of a very popular R&B group. I met him at one of the Hollywood parties. One day, he called me to his tour bus. We sat and chilled for a minute. The next thing I knew, those minutes turned into hours. This was the longest amount of time that I had spent on a bus that wasn't moving. After leaving that bus, that dude was calling me every day.

Back in my early Death Row days, I was young and curious. After my first real sexual encounter with another man, I ended up feeling depressed as hell because it felt so wrong by other people's standards. Being raised in church, I was always told that it was an abomination. I stayed in the crib for weeks after that encounter so that I could make sure that it didn't happen again. That really didn't work for me because I began thinking about it more and more. It was something that I just couldn't shake.

The entertainment business can change you a lot. You could possibly start doing things that you never thought you would do. It's true what they say, once you get money, fame and power; you can do almost anything you want and have anyone you want –male or female. I was able to choose who I slept with. But they had to be a part of the "Crew," meaning, they had to be someone that was as interested in protecting their image as I was. I couldn't risk Suge finding out about my lifestyle.

Chapter 29: A New Love

My roommate Yaku, and I were doing everything we could to get Suge to recognize our music. Suge would sit in the studio with us while we recorded, but real music didn't seem to move him anymore. Dude seemed to have lost touch with both reality and music. I never would have thought in a million years that I would say that. The old Suge was seemingly a genius when it came to music, but this new version was whack. He was a sad shell of the man I once knew.

It wasn't long before I realized that he would never be able to do what he once had. Yaku and I were living in one of Michel'le houses in the valley. We called our place the Pearl House. It's where we recorded. Like always, I kept my door open for my homies when they didn't have a place to stay.

I wasn't living the highlife I once had. There was a daily struggle that I hadn't had with the old Suge. Our checks were slowly disappearing—sometimes they'd come, and other times they wouldn't. Before long, our utilities were getting shut off. I was struggling more than I had when I was in Chicago.

Young Buck was still around. He hadn't bought into any of the shit Ray J was selling. But they were still friends; he maintained a certain loyalty. It was Young Buck that introduced me to Mike "Boog." I left the house early one day, and when I came back, Boog was in the kitchen making a big ass pot of Gumbo—which was the weirdest shit in the world. From that day on, Boog became the little brother I never had. There wasn't a day that went by that he wasn't at the Pearl House.

Two weeks later, we went to his house to meet his mother and father. They immediately felt like family. Before long, we were all cooking and eating together.

One time when Young Buck and I went to Sylmar to pick up Boog, his sister came walking down the stairs. She was dressed up, and on her way to a wedding reception. My eyes followed her every move. I even counted her steps as she walked.

She looked like a black Pocahontas. When she walked into the room, her mother introduced us. When her mom said "Danny, Young Buck, this is Aree," I stood up so fast!

I immediately felt a connection. The only problem was, Buck felt the same thing. When she left the room, Buck said, "I bet I get her first." I'm like, "Bet!"

Before leaving, she came back in the room to say good-bye, she gave me her business card, but she also gave one to Buck. I was mad as hell. When I got into the car, I looked at the picture on the card. Damn. It was like love at first sight.

When I saw Aree again, I told her that she was going to be my wife. The next time we met, she came over to my house. She was there for a pool party. After I had a near-drowning incident, she decided to spend the night. We got in the bed and started kissing; I was easily aroused. But I couldn't do anything, because a few months before I met her, I'd had a bit of an orgy at Pearl house, and I hadn't wrapped up. After getting it in with a couple of sisters, I was hotter than a night in Egypt. After going through that, I was celibate for six months. I was scared to touch anybody, plus I had a lot of respect for her. She was different; she was a church girl.

When she pulled her body close to mine, I started grinding on her. Before things got too far, I jumped out of the bed and on to the floor to stop us from going all the way. It wasn't until a week later that I made love to her for the first time. It was something special.

Things were moving fast with Aree, so I made a call to Chicago to tell Keke that I had found someone that I was interested in. I told her that she had better do something, or else she would lose me forever. Danny Jr. was in town with me at that time. When I told Keke about Aree, she told me that she was coming to California to get her baby *and* her man.

Aree and I were in relationships with other people, but it didn't matter. Our feelings for each other were strong. Aree loved me, and I loved her, and Keke. I was stuck in between two women.

Spiritually, Aree was my soul mate, but I was trying to hang in there for my son. When Keke told me that she was coming to Cali, I didn't believe her. Then early one morning, she called me from LAX. Yaku and I immediately got in his girl's car and went to pick Keke up from the airport. On the way, I called Aree at work to tell her that Keke was in town, and that she would be staying at the house. I told her that I needed some time to see if Keke and I could work things out. She was hurt, but she told me that she'd be waiting for me.

I picked Keke up from the airport and went back to the house. It was nice to see that she was willing to fight for our relationship. Unfortunately, her fight lasted about as long as the sex that we had that night. After we were done, she asked me, "Where is this bitch you talking to?" Before I could say anything to defend Aree, she slapped the shit out of me. When she slapped me, I didn't even fight back. I was ready for her to go back to Chicago. I was ready to get things back on track with Aree, if I still had a chance. The minute that Keke got on the plane, I knew it was over.

Chapter 30: I Found My Good Thing?

Not long after Keke and I broke up, Aree and I were engaged and set to be married. While we were in the midst of planning our wedding, we found out that we would be expecting our first child together. By that time, I had left Pearl house, and was living with Aree and her parents. I thought it was a good idea. They were a model couple, and it gave us an opportunity to see how a successful marriage worked. We had been getting along well, but when Aree finally told her father that she was pregnant, he was mad. "I thought you were smarter than that," he said. I was slightly offended at his statement. Aree already had a son from a previous relationship. She was about to become my wife, I didn't understand his reaction.

My bachelor party was less than stellar. I had expected a wild night out, but with Aree's brother on the team, we ended up going out for beer and wings. It wasn't the night I had envisioned, but I was cool, because I was ready to make Aree my wife.

At our wedding, I sang a song that I had written. It was called "Proposal." I sang the song as Aree came down the aisle. As soon as she came around the corner, she started crying. And as I sang, tears rolled down my face. It was one of the best days of my life; I was marrying my soul mate.

After the ceremony, the wedding party posed for photos. As we were preparing to bless the food, Suge came in with one of his boys. He was holding a white box. Everyone in the hall stopped praying, and watched as he walked over to us. He gave us hugs, and handed the gift to our wedding planner. Suge talked with me briefly, took some pictures with us, and left. Our guest were watching what was going on and taking pictures the whole time Suge was there. Suge enjoyed that attention too! It's funny how he always talked about Puffy wanting to be in the limelight.

Before the reception was over, I went over to see what was in the white box. It was a crystal punch bowl with glasses and spoons.

Everyone was saying how nice it was, but I was thinking, *What the fuck!* It wasn't that I was ungrateful. I just expected something more from my "father." I nearly tore that box apart looking for keys to a house, a deed, a title to a car, or something. I was disappointed to say the least.

Chapter 31: American Idol

My wife was pregnant and just weeks away from giving birth. We were still in our honeymoon phase. We had been living with her parents for a year—trying to decide where we would put down roots. Staying with her parents was ideal for us because we had a chance to save up a little bit of money. I was working as a family counselor at Phoenix Group, a group home for kids.   At all of the jobs that I have ever worked, I never went in giving out my bio, or rattling off a list of things that I had done in my life, but they would eventually find out; maybe it was because I was always singing. The young people that I worked with had all experienced hard lives. It brought joy to my heart to be a part of a staff that was working to steer those young adults in the right direction.

The same year that I worked for the Phoenix Group, I went to San Francisco to audition for American Idol, Season 4. I was contestant number 92346. I slept outside for two nights with about three thousand other aspiring singers. It was another great experience to be out there sleeping on the ground and listening to all kinds of voices singing in line. Though I had been signed to Death Row, my album was never released. I had not yet seen the success I had dreamed of. I was hungry, so I waited with the other hopefuls. We were equals as far as I was concerned.

The next morning, American Idol opened the doors to the arena. People were passing out food, water, toothpaste and juice to each other. It was such an inspiration to see singers going in for what they believed in. We had all slept on the ground, and in the rain for a chance to pass the first set of judges; we wanted to make it to see Simon Cowell, Paula Abdul, and Randy Jackson.

After making it inside, I auditioned for two judges, and advanced to the next round where I sang two songs for the show's producer, Nigel Lythgoe. Once I made it past him, I was on to Simon, Paula and Randy.

When I walked in the room, I was so scared because I saw that Brandy was one of the guest judges. I didn't want her to blow my cover. When I walked in the room, she started jumping up and down. "I know him! That's Danny Boy!" she said.

After that audition, Idol called me and said that I could not be on the show because I had a record deal. But that wasn't the case. I was no longer signed to Death Row, and my album was never released. I did whatever I could to downplay the whole Death Row thing. By some miracle, my plan worked, and they agreed to let me compete. At work, the staff and clients hung banners in support of me.

Idol checked the contestants into a hotel. At this juncture, we no longer had to sleep outside. During this time, I had the chance to meet a lot of good singers and people from all over the world. When it was time to be put in groups, I was paired with two other guys. Scott Salvo was from Ohio, and Matthew Myers was from Georgia. After the first day, I knew that our team was at risk because Scott had an attitude with Matthew and I. It was like he thought that he was too good to sing with us. When we were scheduled for rehearsal, Scott would show up late. Not only did we have to learn the songs, we had to come up with a routine, and none of us knew how to dance. Both of my group mates were talented singers, and our voices melded together beautifully. If they were judging solely based on our vocal ability, we would have nothing to worry about.

The next day they had us sitting in the arena for a long time before they even began filming. We sat there and waited nervously until it was our time to perform. When we got on the stage, Matthew forgot some of his verse. That made me nervous as hell. When I came out to do my part, I didn't feel that I did as well as I wanted. Scott sung the last verse, and we ended the song with a hard harmony.

After performing, Randy and Paula said that it was the best harmonic ending that they had ever heard on the show. At the end of it, I was really happy with what we had done. After all of the performances were complete, all of the contestants that performed were told if they had made it to the next round. From our group, Scott and I had made it through, but Matthew was cut. I felt really bad for Matthew because he was really cool.

Things progressed fast after the cut. It seemed as though they were trying to put a lot more pressure on the artists that were left. I hung in there. With each performance, the judges would give me a great compliment.

Things were going well until Idol's lawyer came to me with copies of the Death Row website. I was all over the site, along with promotional copy about my album release. The lawyer walked up to me and was like, "What the fuck is this?" And he walked away. By this time, they placed different groups in different rooms. I didn't think anything of it because all of the people that were in the room that I was in could sing their asses off. After sitting in the room for a while, the judges came in and announced that our group would be going home.

I was at a loss for words. I felt that I had missed out on another opportunity to share with the world. Death Row had me at a standstill once again, but life, and music goes on.

* I'm not a hater or anything, but how the hell did Scott make it so far?

Chapter 32: Where Do We Go From Here?

Aree and I took a trip to Chicago so that she could have a chance to meet the family and friends that were unable to make it to LA for our wedding. We were also on the hunt for a family home, so we scheduled an appointment with a realtor so that we could explore the Chicago market. We saw some nice houses, but after braving the bitter cold, we decided to take our home search elsewhere. When the holidays were over, we were on our way back to sunny LA.

Aree had a friend who had been going back and forth between Atlanta and California. She had finally found a property that she wanted, and her house was being built. She had hyped it up, so we decided to have a look for ourselves. When we arrived in Atlanta, we met up with the same agent that helped Aree's friend find her place. By the time we headed back to California, our house was being built.

In no time, we were shopping for furniture and moving into our house. The house had a huge kitchen and living room. The master suite was the size of a one-bedroom apartment. Atlanta was a good move for us. We both had great jobs. And I had partnered with her father to open a picture and home décor store. Business was good with so many people relocating to Georgia.

We lived in Atlanta for a few years without family. That was really hard on us. My stepson, David was missing his grandparents. Damarion was a baby when we moved to Atlanta, and so he hadn't really had a chance to know them.

When the economy failed, everything went crazy. Aree was laid off, and my job wasn't paying enough to keep us afloat. Business slowed, so we had no choice but to close our store.

Just about every other month, Aree's dad had to help us out financially. With the cost of living in California becoming more expensive, her parents decided to relocate to Atlanta. This way they would be closer to the children, and together we would be able to make things work financially.

Many people had told me that it was a bad idea, but I had lived with Aree's family before. I didn't think we'd have a problem.

Chapter 33: Trouble in Paradise

The first sign of trouble came before Aree's parents had even made it to Georgia. Her father was demanding the master bedroom. He told her that he would not come unless we gave it to him. I told her to tell him to stay in California if that was the case. I wasn't letting anybody move into that room. By this time, I should have seen what everyone was talking about, but I guess I had to find out for myself.

Aree and I were already having problems; we were barely getting along, because we were having serious financial problems. People tend to forget about the good times when finances go awry. To make matters worse, my back problems had returned; I could barely walk. The pain made it hard for me to find consistent work.

When my in-laws arrived, I did everything I could to make sure they were comfortable. I treated them the same way I would have treated my own parents if they were there, but their timing couldn't have been worse; Aree and I were really going through. We weren't kissing, and there was no sex. We were barely communicating. Usually we would talk several times a day. Even my stepson stopped communicating with me as he normally did. Things were falling apart, but we were trying to work them out.

Within four months, things had change drastically. I was feeling like I was living with a family that I was not a part of. My wife had started going out with her friends all the time, and I was going in and out of town, sometimes out of the country chasing after this music thing. Our marriage was holding on by a string. The tension in the house was thick.

When I left for my gigs in Amsterdam, my father-in-law was working on a model train set. It was the size of a twin bed. That train set took up over half of the guest room, but that wasn't as bad as the Blockbuster Movie store he had set up in the same room. He had installed shelves, and organized his movies in alphabetical order. There were at least three thousand VHS tapes in his collection. As crazy as it was, I offered a compromise. I told my wife that he could have the recording booth that I had built in the garage to store his tapes, but he complained that the climate would damage his collection.

When I returned from my gig in Amsterdam, I was looking for my cat. His name was Studio. When I couldn't find Studio, I started looking for his litter pan. When my son came home from school, I asked him where the cat was. He said, "Grandpa gave it to the lady." I called Aree cursing like a motherfucker. When we talked, she said, "I didn't want the cat anyway." My father-in-law had taken over my house, and I had let it happen.

I couldn't say anything to Aree because her father could do nothing wrong in her eyes. He knew what he was doing, because the more she and I fell out, the more silent he became with me. I felt like he was trying to be her husband and her father. He was trying to do everything I was doing.

When I talked to her mother about our problems, she would say, "It will be ok." After a while, that changed into "Maybe you all should separate if that's what she wants."

Aree had been telling me that she didn't want to be married anymore. She said that I didn't have enough to offer. She felt that I was taking from my other children; she needed more. She wanted me to leave our family home, but I didn't want that. I tried marriage counseling, but by that point, it didn't matter to Aree what anybody had to say when it came to making the marriage work.

I had nowhere to go. I packed my truck as much as I could, but the majority of my things went into the trash, and walked away from my wife, my sons, and my life. Everything I had dreamed of was gone.

I slept in my truck for about two weeks. I would stop in at LA Fitness to shower.

When I left, my mind wasn't right. I didn't know whether I wanted to hurt myself or someone else. I didn't want to live anymore. Some nights I prayed to die.

My boy Parrish came up on a studio during the same time that I was going through. It was a five-bedroom house. Back in the Chi, we would call that a baby mansion. The house was damn near ready for MTV's Cribs.

Being that I had no work, and nowhere to stay, Parrish worked out a deal with the owner to allow me to stay at the studio house while I fixed it up. I was working day and night painting, cutting grass, dumping trash, laying tile, and patching holes; I did whatever needed to be done.

Parrish and I had plans to open up the studio to artists and record companies. I had already started to take on clients. There were even some producers and engineers that were getting involved, but the house was taking forever to complete.

Late one night, I sat in that very house and contemplated suicide. The problem was, I was too scared to die, and too smart to kill myself. Once again, I was feeling sorry for myself. My life had been a series of highs and lows, and I couldn't imagine my future.

The spirit of God came to me that night saying, "Look around. What do you mean you don't have anything?" It was a revelation for me. I had been complaining about my circumstances, not realizing that despite all the things I had been through, God had always kept me.

Chapter 34: Dearly Departed

While things were falling apart in Atlanta, I got the news that my sister Linda had suffered a stroke. It took me a while to come up with the money to go back home, but I called to check on her every day. The stroke had messed up her speech, but she was eventually released from the hospital. Whenever I talked to her, she would cry because I couldn't understand what she was saying. She had been so used to saying whatever she wanted, whenever she wanted. It was a harsh reality. And it reminded me of how my mother suffered.

I never really realized how sick my sister Linda was. Before long, she suffered another stroke. This time, her brain swelled and she had blot clots; it was devastating. While Linda was in the hospital fighting for her life, Kimberla's father, my uncle Junior, was in hospice, preparing to make his transition.

Kimberla and I made the drive to Chicago to see her father. While I was driving, Kim fell asleep. We were about two hours away from Chicago when my phone rang. It was my Aunt Joanne. Kimberla's father had died. She told me not to say anything to Kimberla, so I didn't. It was one of the hardest rides of my life. I knew how close Kimberla and her dad were. I just wished we had made it there in time enough for her to say good-bye.

While arrangements were being made for Uncle Junior, I went to the rehabilitation center to see Linda. It messed me up to see her laying in the bed with tubes down her throat; she didn't even know I was there. I grabbed her hand, but she could not grip my hand at all. There was a sense of emptiness, but I was still hoping and praying that she would pull through.

After the funeral, I went back home to Atlanta. I wasn't there a month before Linda passed away. No matter how many people I lost, I could never get used to death. It always knocked the wind out of me. Losing my sister broke my heart.

When I went back to Chicago, I went alone. It hurt my heart to travel alone. I couldn't believe that Aree wasn't with me. At the service, everyone was asking, "Where is your wife?"

I had experienced death in so many ways; I had lost so many people that were close to me. If I ever needed someone by my side, it was then. I felt like I was in a lonely battle. True enough, I had family and friends, but I needed my wife; I needed her shoulder to cry on. I wanted to lie on the pillow and talk to her until we feel asleep.

Linda's death hit our family hard. It was unbelievable to us that she was gone. Her death brought the family closer together. I always made sure that I talked to my sister, Orlean on most Sunday's. We made sure that we called each other on holidays and on Mama's birthday. We always called each other on our birthdays as well. We'd been doing that since our mom passed.

My sister Renee would always call me. If I didn't answer, she would leave a message on my phone telling me that she loved me. Renee had lived in Detroit since I was a little boy. She would send for my mom and I every Thanksgiving. We would always take Greyhound; it was something that my mom and I looked forward to.

*****

Every now and then, I would be on the road with a fellow by the name of Norman Connors. The gigs didn't pay much, but I was staying in five-star hotels. I was singing, and I had a roof over my head. It was a step up from sleeping in my truck.

The pay was so low that sometimes I spent more getting to the shows and eating than I made from the performance. Sometimes I had nothing at all. Norman always came up with an excuse. It was like I was doing shows for a crack head promoter. But he wasn't on crack. He was just a bad businessman. After a while, I refused to take calls from him until he got his shit together.

Whenever I was doing badly, my sister Peaches would help. I would only call her when I had exhausted all of my other options. One time, I was on the side of the road, about to run out of gas. My sister loaded money on a Green Dot card, and I was able to get food and gas.

Renee called me one Saturday to invite me to her birthday party. During this time, my car wasn't working. Before I was able to get the car out of the shop, I got a call from my sister Orlean telling me that Renee had suffered a massive stroke. She was in intensive care. *Not again!* I couldn't believe it was happening again. It would be a week before I'd be able to drive up to Detroit. Before I could leave Atlanta, Renee suffered another stroke and had to have emergency brain surgery.

Seeing her brought back so many memories of my mother. It didn't help that her hospital wristband read *"Dorothy R. Steward."* We called her Renee, but that was her middle name. She had actually been named after our mother. It was hard to take.

Renee's head was visibly swollen when I saw her. By the next day, it was nearly three times that size. She was going through the same thing my sister Linda had. The day after, I went to the hospital, but before I entered the room, I was warned about what I would see. Renee was in this special bed that was supposed to help remove the fluid from her lungs. It looked like a huge casket. She was strapped to the bed, lying on the side, in mid-air. Her condition was grave, and it was hard to watch her suffer like that.

The family needed to come together and make some decisions, because the doctors had done all they could do. On October 2nd, my son DJ's birthday, we all arrived at the hospital, and watched as she took her very last breath.

Every time I thought about her, I would see a vision of that machine counting down. I just could not believe this shit. I had faith in God, but this I just didn't understand.

I felt cursed. I had lost two sisters and an uncle in the same year.

Chapter 35: Amsterdam Loves Danny Boy

When I came back to Atlanta, I was broke and alone. I had started living with a guy, but that situation wasn't working out. Soon, I was going back and forth between Atlanta and Kimberla's home in Knoxville. I was leading praise and worship at a local church, but it felt like just a job. I was missing my own church. I needed to hear a word from Pastor Pollard.

My soul felt empty. My life, my faith, my confidence, and my trust were low. Sometimes I really didn't' know which way to go. I didn't know how to fix the relationships that had been broken, and I couldn't make up for the time that I missed in my children's lives.

I had been separated for Aree for a full year. And many things had changed. I was no longer hurt about our separation. I was focused on my relationship with my son. I grew to understand that some relationships were only for a season. In the words of the Whisper's, "The beat goes on…"

Over the years, I had formed a friendship with artists and promoters in Amsterdam. I was always well received. In Amsterdam, I experienced a level of success that I hadn't in the states. The first time I went to Amsterdam was to do a benefit concert that Mama Janette put together for the Malocan prisoners. What began as a one-time trip, soon turned into an annual event. Each year, I would fly into Amsterdam and share my gift of song.

It was during my first visit to Amsterdam that I found a Café Today. It was a place where I could enjoy some of its finest herbs. There, I could finally relax and ease my mind.

Amsterdam was so liberal. It didn't matter what people's lifestyle choice was; they were human. No one cared if I smoked weed; they didn't care if I was gay, or bisexual.

Amsterdam was good for me. I would always hear people playing Tupac's music. It amazed me that I could meet people from so far away from home and that shared the same love for Pac's music as people back in the states. I wish

Pac would have had a chance to see how many people he influenced, and how many lives he touched

I had been in Amsterdam for a couple weeks when I was dealt another blow. Marcus, my childhood friend, had been murdered in Chicago. I was listening to Frank Sinatra when I got a message on Facebook: *"Give Cicely a call, her brother passed last night."* I was crushed. Marcus and I had known each other since grade school. He had been so supportive of my career. During the times he was locked up, he would call me from jail and ask me to sing. I would sing for the other inmates too. By the time we got off the phone, I would have done a full concert. Losing him hurt like hell.

I couldn't make it to Marcus' funeral. I wanted to be there; I was supposed to be there. He was my brother. On the day of his service, I stayed in the house all day and I cried every time I thought about what I was missing at the funeral. Perhaps it was better that I wasn't there. Whenever I closed my eyes and imagined him in that casket, it would take me to a dark place. Just knowing how strong our brotherhood was, gives me comfort. I know that we will meet again.

Chapter 36: Blood, Sweat & Tears

When I got back to Atlanta, it was around the holidays. I was happy to be back in the states, but I didn't have anywhere to stay. I had a friend who told me that I could stay with him. When he found out that I was struggling, he offered to help me. It was the first time that a guy was there for me in that way. He was a nurturer. George met me at the airport, and took me back to his place in Buckhead. By this time, I had been with a few men, but I was still on the down low; I was hiding. But we were living at The Darlington. It was a building that was a known hangout for gay men. Things started out sweet, but by the time the holidays had passed, we were over.

February 7, 2011

Ever since my mom's passing, February 7th had been a hard day for me. I thought it might help if I got high. One of my friends had a pill that he called a *bean*, I decided that I would pop one to try and suppress the pain I was feeling, but the pill made me paranoid; I felt like I was on a roller coaster. When I finally came down, I slept hard. I didn't wake up until the next afternoon.

February 8, 2011

I slept the morning away. When I finally woke up, it was almost 3p.m. I couldn't get out of bed to save my own life. When I got up and looked at my phone, I noticed that I had a ton of missed calls and messages, all from Chicago numbers. I called the number of the last missed call; it was my sister, Tina. When she answered, the first thing she said was "Boy we've been trying to call you all day! Your daddy dead." It was like I was in a dream. I really couldn't believe what she was telling me. I hung up the phone, and called my sister Peaches. My dad had been living with her.

When my nephew, Greg answered the phone, he started crying before I could even ask. It was true. My father had passed away on the same day as my mother had seventeen years prior. To make matters worse, it was Greg's birthday. I felt like I was living in a nightmare. *How could something like this be happening?* Once again, I started making plans to leave Atlanta. I felt like I was about to lose my mind. I was grieving both of my parents at the same time.

When I arrived at the airport, I could see my sister's bright smile from a distance. Peaches and I were my father's only children, though my father happily raised all of my mother's children. When I got to her, she had tears rolling down her face. I hated seeing my sister like that because she had always been the one to stop me from crying. I wanted to be there for her, but I couldn't get myself together.

When we sat down to plan my father's funeral, we were hit with another blow. His insurance had been canceled because they were unable to withdraw the monthly payment. My sister could see my despair. It hurt that I couldn't afford to bury my father. "Don't worry. We gone do what need to be done for daddy," she said. "Don't worry about a thing."

As we moved forward with the arrangements, we hit another snag. There was no one to eulogize my father. The preachers that knew him were too "Spiritual" to speak over my father. Even people in my family said no. My father was a good guy who was rooted in the community. He was always willing to help people out. It was sad that no one felt compelled to speak for a man who had given so much of himself. Theology aside, he was a child of God. As we went about looking for a pastor, someone suggested that my sister and I deliver the eulogy. It was decided. We would do just that. At the end of the day, I realized that it was all a part of the Master's plan.

All of the studying and preparing that I had done that whole week had gone out the window. I couldn't remember a thing. I couldn't read a thing off the paper. God just showed up and spoke through me. I was used as a vessel to give a word to the people.

When we got up to speak for our father, we did our best to honor his memory. I had always dreamed of giving my first sermon, looking out into the audience of people, and seeing my daddy smiling back at me. I never would have imagined that I would be doing it at his funeral. I always prayed that he'd have the opportunity to hear me. And though my daddy was no longer there in flesh, God fixed it so that he could hear me preach. It was church in the most untraditional way. I believe that somebody was saved that day. It's amazing how God works.

After my father's death, I started working with my friend at his new Jazz club and bar. That's where I met Robert. When I met him, I told him that I was going to kidnap him. After about a week or so, that's just what I did. My relationship with Robert was my first serious relationship with a man. We would spend all of our free time together. But soon that would come to an end. When we broke up, it was hard for me to shake.

Chapter 37: Grandma Williams

My cousin wrote me on Facebook and informed me that Grandma Williams had passed away. She told me that my uncle was the one that discovered her. Mrs. Williams wasn't my grandmother by birth, but she never treated me any different than her own grandchildren. I was a part of her family. I had even lived with in the years before I was sentenced to Death Row. She had so much to do with the man I grew to become.

When the family asked me to deliver her eulogy, I was both afraid and elated. It was an honor. Despite the occasion, I was glad to be home. It was a dark time in my life, and I needed to be around my family and friends. I needed to be around people who loved me. I ended up staying in Chicago that entire summer.

Had it not been for my cousin Esha and her husband Quincy, I wouldn't have had a dime in my pocket. They gave me a job working for their moving company. I was going out just about every day moving furniture, boxes, pianos; you name it. If it was moveable, I moved it.

As the summer came to an end, I felt like I had worn out my welcome. My godfather had been trying to get me to come to Ohio for a while. It would give me an opportunity to mellow out before I returned to Atlanta. My godfather had spent much of his life in the music business. In fact, that's how we met. When I was on the road with Norman Connors, Pops took me under his wing. He was sort of an adopted godfather.

Chapter 38: Welcome to Cleveland

When I arrived at Pop's house, his wife welcomed me in with open arms. They had a room waiting for me; it was a nice set up. That house was anointed. Mama Jean is a praying, and anointed woman of God. It was great to be in her company. I even accompanied her and Pops to their church. They were Adventists, and went to church on Saturday. It was a new experience, and I enjoyed it!

I was still trying to shake my breakup. I had failed relationships before, but this was different. I was in Cleveland for two months before I met Anthony. I enjoyed his company. And for the first time in a long time, I wasn't thinking about my previous relationship. We connected online first. Once we met in person, we were together almost every day.

I called Anthony one day to tell him that I would pick him up from work. Before I hung up the phone, he said, "Ok Bae. I love you." I was shocked. The only thing I could get out of my mouth was, "Alright see you in a minute." It was as if Anthony knew that his time was limited. When I was with him, he tried to give me every bit of him. We talked about everything. He easily made me feel secure with all my insecurities. Everything that I was uncomfortable about, he slowly erased. I even took my socks off in front of him.

We would lay up at night and talk about everything. He shared with me how he was hurt from his childhood. He talked about how his family had accepted the fact that he was gay, but that he also felt different and distant from them.

He was down because he had lost a good job at Nestle due to an accident at work. He was helping a lady move a table when it landed on someone's foot. They gave him a drug test and found weed in his system. They suspended him for a few days, and then eventually let him go. That bothered him so much. I just didn't realize how much it did.

A few days after the Thanksgiving Holiday, Anthony and I were walking to the store. He told me that sometimes he just didn't feel like being alive. When he told me that his father had committed suicide when he was a toddler, I immediately asked him how he felt right then. Before he could give me an answer, I grabbed his hand in the middle of the parking lot, in three inches of snow, and began to pray. "You met the right nigga," I told him. I stood there and interceded on his behalf. He told me that he loved me because I was so spiritual.

At this time, I was preparing to go back out on the road with Norman Connors. We were scheduled to do a show in Jacksonville, FL. It was only paying about three hundred dollars, but I was doing what I loved. Plus Kimberla had moved to Jacksonville and I was looking forward to seeing her.

The Thursday before my trip, Anthony and I had the chance to spend time together. I made us a dinner of steak, potatoes and spinach. When the food was all done and we began to eat, he looked up at me and said, "Damn baby, you can cook too?" We ate good, smoked a nice one, and laid-up all night watching movies, kissing, hugging, and…what rhymes with hugging?

While we hung out that night, someone came to the door and started ringing the bell. Anthony told me to ignore it, but the person kept coming back every hour. Every time I asked him to answer the door, he would say that he wasn't expecting anyone. Whoever it was, they stayed on that bell 'til 5am.

At one point, I looked out of the window and saw someone in a hoodie. I couldn't see his face, but I could see the smoke from his breath as he stood there in the cold. It was an eerie sight. I couldn't imagine why someone would be so committed that they would stay out in the cold for hours waiting for someone.

Early the next morning, as I prepared to go to the airport, Anthony helped me get my things together. He was smiling and kissing all over me. He seemed so happy. As happy as I was to be with him, I was excited to be leaving that cold ass weather. My cousin Kimberla had moved to Florida, and I couldn't wait to see her.

As soon as my plane landed in Florida, I talked to Anthony. He was so worried that I wasn't coming back because he knew how bad I wanted to get back to Atlanta. Little did he know, I was actually looking forward to getting back to Cleveland to be with him.

Chapter 39: Love Against Suicide & Hate

Jacksonville, FL

When I got to Florida, I was walking around in shorts; I was happy to be out of the cold. I couldn't wait for sound check so that I could hit the stage. I was happy to see Norman and the crew. It had been a while since we'd done a gig together. I was glad to be back in my element. The show started slow, but when the crowd began to sing along, things fell right into place. It was a great show! I was happy to see Kimberla out there supporting me like she had back in the day.

We did two shows that night. When I got back to the hotel that night, the first thing I did was plug my phone into the charger. When it powered up, I saw that I had missed Anthony's call at about 2 am. I tried to call him back, but he didn't answer. I kept trying to call him until I eventually fell asleep.

I was up at 6:45 the next morning getting ready to go to the airport to make my 9:45 flight. When I got to the airport, I found out that my flight back to Cleveland had been canceled because of the snowstorm. I hung out with Kimberla until I could find another flight out.

When I got word that there was another flight that could possibly get me back to Cleveland, I went back to the airport. I wasn't at the airport an hour before I got a call from Anthony's phone, but it wasn't him. It was his brother. His voice was trembling. "My brother killed himself last night," he said. I looked at the phone to make sure that it was really Anthony's number. "My brother Anthony killed himself last night. He hung himself," he repeated. I was at a loss of words; my heart dropped. I was in the middle of the airport, but I felt like I had been transported to another place. It was like all of the walls were closing in on me. Once I came to my senses, I called Kim. When she answered, she could tell right away that something wasn't right. "What's wrong Danny," she said. I asked her to come right away. I didn't know what else to do. Shock and confusion took over. I stood outside of the airport like something from the "Twilight Zone." I was in a zombie-like state when Kim pulled up.

Once I had a chance to gather myself, I called Anthony's best friend. When she answered the phone, she was crying hysterically. She told me that she had just seen Anthony; he had come to her job to finish his homework.

She told me how much Anthony loved me, and how he couldn't wait until I came back. She said the he acted as if he was fine. "I can't believe it," she said.

I called Anthony's mom and talked to her. She said that she would wait for me to return before she made any plans. After I got off the phone with Anthony's mom, I went to Facebook and posted a status: *"Finally feeling somebody and they committed suicide #wow #RIPToni.* My page immediately blew up with messages of condolences. Some of the messages read, *"Praying for her and her family."* and *"May she rest in peace."*

I boarded a flight back to Ohio the same day. When I arrived in Cleveland, Pops picked me up and took me to Anthony's family home. When I saw Anthony's mom and the rest of his family, reality really set in.

His family talked about how much Anthony and I looked alike. They also told me how much they had heard about me. Whenever I was introduced, it was as the person that Anthony was dating.

As we sat around and talked, more details about his death were revealed. It was his sister and her boyfriend that discovered Anthony's body.

She said that when they walked into the apartment, it was dark and cold. The windows were cracked despite the fact that it was 30 degrees below zero outside.

When they noticed how quiet it was in the house, Anthony's sister walked to his room and knocked on the door. The door to the room was hollow, but his sister could feel his weight on the door. When she pushed against it, and felt the body weight at the door, she took off running, and never entered the room.

When her boyfriend went to the room, and attempted to open the door, he could tell that something was jammed behind it. He used his shoulder to nudge the door open, and it barely moved. He forced it open as far as he could. Through the crack, he was able to squeeze through the opening to get into the room.

He found Anthony hanging from the hinge of the door. He had hung himself with a necktie. He took him down as quickly as he could, but it was too late. Rigor mortis had already set in.

When Anthony died, he had been going through a lot. He was feeling the weight of the world on his shoulders. After losing his job, bills began to pile up. His weed guy had grown persistent, and wasn't letting up. When word of Anthony's death reached the streets, his weed guy was one of the first to show up. I told the detectives about the person I had seen in the parking lot, but they saw no signs of forced entry. I was furious. I couldn't believe that Anthony, my friend, my lover had taken his own life.

From what I heard, Anthony told his mom how much he liked me. I guess that really held weight with her because she told me that Anthony never really liked anyone that much. She told me that she wanted me to help make the arrangements. "Out of respect for our relationship," she said. She even asked me how I would like to be mentioned in the program.

When we were ready to go into the back to see his body, so many emotions flooded my body. My eyes began to water, and my inside began to tremble. As we walked toward the door of the room where Anthony's body was being held, it was like walking down the hall to the gas chamber. It was almost like the feeling of knowing that you are going to meet your demise and there's nothing you can do about it.

When they finally saw Anthony's lifeless body, the family broke down. My eyes flooded with tears. The last time I had seen him, he was alive and well.

The family left me alone to have a moment with Anthony. When I tried to walk up to look at him, I could barely walk. He didn't look the same. Anthony's skin was darkened, and his body was swollen. I looked to see if there were signs of a struggle. Even though the investigators ruled it a suicide, I still didn't want to believe that he had done this to himself. In the end, I had to come to grips that he in fact took his own life.

I went back to Facebook and posted another status that read: "RIP Anthony." I wanted to get some financial help from my Facebook family to help with arrangements. One of the comments left on the status said, *"Man Bro!!"* another read *"Damn, You knew two people that committed suicide this week?"* My response to that comment was, "This was the person I was dating." In the time after I made that post, I had received over twelve hundred messages, comments, and likes.

One of the messages read, "*What the Fuck! If Pac was alive he would kill yo bitch ass.*" People began to question if my page had been hacked, and if someone was trying to demean me. One message read, "*What the fuck you saying? You gay?*"

"Naw, I'm bisexual," I replied.

Over the next days, I caught a lot of flak from my family. Some of them were supportive, but others made hurtful comments. It was a hard time. I was grieving Anthony, and people were trying their best to break me down even further.

On the day of the service, I was in bad shape. I had been crying all day. Pops knew about my sexuality, but Mama Jean didn't. All she knew was that I had lost a good friend.

Mama Jean was supposed to go to work that day but didn't because she said she wanted to be a support to me and go to the funeral. She wanted to make sure that I was going to be okay. I was so nervous. I really didn't want her to go. I knew this is the first time that I would be "out" publicly, and it was going to happen at this funeral.

When we arrived at the service, the family was preparing to walk in. Mama Jean was by my side the whole time. When she walked down the aisle and up to the casket with me, she kept a tight squeeze on my arm. I was seated in the row with the family, directly behind Anthony's parents. Mama Jean sat right next to me the whole time and didn't ask any questions.

When the service began, the directors asked Anthony's mom if she wanted the casket opened or closed during the service. She directed them to come ask me. When the directors came to me and asked, I was kind of confused. I look to her for confirmation, and she gave me a nod of approval. I wanted the casket open.

When I got up to speak, I shared the details of a conversation I had with Anthony:

"What do you think God thinks about gay people?" he asked.

My response was, "John 3:16, For God so loved the world that he gave his only begotten son, that whosoever believes in him should not perish…"

And that's where I left it.

Anthony's untimely death led me to start my non-profit, "Love Against Suicide and Hate."

Chapter 40: Living Out Loud

After Anthony's untimely death, my life changed. I made the choice to no longer try to hide in the shadows of who I was. I decided that my life would not be worth living if I was living to please other people.

What was sad about it was that it took Anthony's death to give me life. His death allowed me to muster up the courage to be me. So I made the decision to live out loud.

There were many people that didn't like it. I just dealt with the bull as it came. Please believe me… questions and comments are still coming, and I am still being condemned. I must admit…this is a hard thing to deal with at times because of the views and opinions of others about my sexuality.

People always have an opinion about someone if they are Lesbian, Gay, Bi-sexual or Transgender. I've lost plenty of friends. People that had respect for me prior to knowing about my sexual orientation began to disrespect me. I realize that not everyone can deal with it, but I wonder if it might be due to their own insecurities. Who knows?

There are times that I regret "coming out." I guess if I hadn't, I wouldn't have to deal with the drama, lying, and whorish-ass niggas that come along with it. What bothers me the most is the thought of people not wanting to hear me or support me because of it.

Spiritually, I'm ok because I learned that it's not about what man thinks about me. After going through everything I've been through, and survived, I've gained a relationship with God for myself.

John 3:16 says, *"For God so love the world that he gave his only begotten son that who so ever believe in him shall not perish but have ever lasting life."*

One thing I can attest to is that I love the Lord; I am a believer. I know that he died for me and there's nothing anyone can do to separate me from his blood. Let me help you understand what I'm saying by this example: When blood get on your clothes, notice, no matter what you do...you can't wash it away. Aren't you glad to know God doesn't just throw us away? I'm glad that I'm a living testimony. That's why I'm going to do my best to share my music, my voice, my words and my testimony with the world. There are so many people hurt from tragedies and experiences of their past. They feel stuck, stagnated, and far away from God.

I'm glad I'm able to spread God's love, one person at a time! Well, at least that's my goal. I'm really glad things are changing and people are becoming less judgmental or should I say more accepting to the idea of "allowing" people to love who they want.

My life mission is to please God, my creator, and try my best to be Christ like while I'm breathing and alive on this Earth. I can't imagine leaving this place, and not making it to heaven.

The thing I don't want is for my kids to hurt because of the choices I've made. I hope that they understand. I hope that my orientation doesn't change the way my sons see me.

And I definitely don't want to persuade or mislead them in

anyway. They are handsome young guys, and I can't wait to

see them date, go to prom, get married, and have their own

little Danny Boys running around!

Chapter 41: I Am Danny Boy

I last saw Afeni Shakur when the Tupac museum opened in Atlanta. When she saw me, she looked as if she had seen a ghost. I was the last person she expected to see. It looked like the air had left her body. When she regained her composure, she came over and gave me a hug. "This is how we keep Tupac alive," she said to me. "You are welcomed here." Then she got into her car, and rode away. She was playing on my emotions.

I didn't expect a check that day, but I hoped that there would be some communication. She had talked about Suge like he was a monster, but when it came down to it, she was worse. She knew what it was like to fight for what was right, but still she left me with nothing. She even took me off of some of the songs that I had recorded with Pac. They used Jon B in place of me. When I met him, he told me that he had followed my voice, word for word; he had matched every run.

What Afeni owed me was minute in relation to what she received from the estate. She knew how much I had contributed to the album, and to his legacy. Even today, if I want to download the "I Ain't Mad At Cha" ringtone, I have to pay for it. It doesn't even have Pac's parts on it—just my voice. I was watching Alpha Dog one night and I heard "Toss it Up" playing. It was during the scene where Justin Timberlake was dancing at a party. It was on my verse; not a dime of that money comes to me.

When people die, we tend to put them on pedestals. We only want to remember the good stuff, but I know another side. When Afeni died, she left a bill; she left here owing me. And it's not just for me. It's my children's birthright. It's sad when anyone dies, but it didn't have to be like that with us.

The industry has a dark side. And I experienced that with many people, Michel'le being one of them. I've seen her biopic. It seemed like she wanted to make Dre look bad. I came around long after NWA, so there was some stuff shown that I wasn't there to witness. I'm never for a man putting his hands on a woman, but what I'm saying is that Michel'le should never be put on a pedestal; she was a devil. She wasn't innocent; she went from Dre to Suge, and made sure that Suge eventually had a problem with everyone on Death Row. She didn't want anyone closer to him than her, and it paid off. She was like that person who would pinch your baby when you weren't looking. Yeah, she pinched a lot of niggas.

When Keyshia Cole and I reconnected recently, I was initially ecstatic. But she quickly severed our ties when she tried to screw me over for what amounted to some pocket change for her. As long as I live, I will never understand how the rich can so brazenly take advantage of the poor.

As much as I felt screwed over, I also felt the love. The last time I saw Mary J, she was at her CD signing. When she saw me, she screamed, and rushed me into her limo. She was as passionate as ever. Till this day, Mary could still get it! I'd have my boyfriend in the next room. I'd say to him, "You better not say nothing! Nigga that's Mary!" That's my baby. I love her.

I have been in the music industry in some shape or form for over two decades. During that time, I have made many memories that I wouldn't trade for the world. I've performed with legends, and seen many of those people transition. Even today, people recognize me for the work I did with Tupac. It was a great time. I've been doing music long enough to prove my staying power. And I have enough faith to believe that my time is here. I was born for this. I am Danny Boy.

Acknowledgements

It has taken me over six years to write this book. I hope that you have learned about the life, lies and legacy of hip-hop. Well, Some of them. I hope that I have answered some of the burning questions you've always had about the time I spent on Death Row with Suge Knight and Tupac.

This book was written with the hope that it would inspire. I hope that someone can learn from the many mistakes I made in my musical career and personal life.

For those of you that are surprised about some of the things I have revealed, I hope it wears off, and you feel better soon! I feel better now that you know; the weight has been lifted. You know all about me, well the parts I've chosen to share! I've opened up my diary, and given you backstage access.

To my homies, I hope y'all understand where I'm coming from, and I hope my sexuality, or sexual preference doesn't ruin our friendship. If it does, I question our "friendship" in the first place. Please also understand that just because I have my preferences, there is not a friend I have that I like…or have thought about in that way. We're cool!

To the ladies, I hope you all can understand and respect my new honesty in the matter. I still love women physically, and sexually. If you get down with me, you know what it is! Catch me on Instagram, Facebook, hell…Google me!

To my family, I hope you can love me through it all! I just want you all to love me no matter what my choices are. I hope to never bring embarrassment or shame to our family for choices I have made, but it's time for Danny Boy to live for Danny Boy, with as much respect to my family as I can give. I pray that we can learn to forgive and move on in love…like families were made to do.

Daddy, before you passed on, it was my hope that you would only read this part. Rest well, Daddy (Blood); take care of mama!

I would like to thank God, my father, my friend, my Savior, who is the head of my household... Thank you for keeping and sustaining me, for a time like this... Thanks for choosing me, and thanks for lending me the gifts of music and speaking.... I promise to take care of them.

To my children:

Ashlee.... I love you so much. You will always be my baby girl. Thank for understating me and loving me through it all.... I see so much in you.... Just know your daddy will always be here for you.

Kai.... I love you baby girl...

Danny Boy Jr.–DJ…Son, I love and miss u so much... I can't apologize enough for all the time I missed. But one thing is for sure, when we have an opportunity to fix it... I'll never let a day go… Keep balling. I watch you all the time at a distance, can't wait for the chance to be up Close... You're my junior, my namesake... I love you son.

Quanny man... I'm still yo daddy ... Love u son.

Damarion...Baby boy.... Thanks for always lifting my spirit... You're such an amazing kid...wouldn't trade you for the world... Can't wait for all of us to travel the world.

David...son I love you... glad you stayed in LA. I got kids everywhere now! Lol.

To the mothers of my Nations:

Katrina, I love you. Thanks for being a friend... Your understanding and friendship is invaluable... Long as I'm breathing, you will never want for nothing, if I got it... So tell your future husband I'm always coming over. Lol.

Katicha, I pray for the day that you forgive me for whatever it is that I've done wrong... I've known you since 4th grade, I have no choice but to love you...one day we will look back on this and laugh... I looked forward to co-parenting with you

Aree, thanks for the experience of love, marriage, and that talented lil boy of ours... Look forward to a lot of games and shows...

To Pastor Pollard & First Lady (Gabb and Daniel)...Pastor thanks for your wisdom, your spiritual guidance, and love... When I had no family in Atlanta, y'all took me in as if y'all had known me a million years....

To my church family, Enon, thanks for supporting and loving me, and know that I am a work in progress; God is not finished with me yet. I'm still under construction!

To my sister's and brothers:

I love y'all so much and can't wait to make it so we can build a legacy...Tina, Orlean, Celestine, Anthony, and Zack.

Rip Linda Steward

Rip Renee Steward

To my aunt's:

Lois, thanks for music and your sweet spirit. Aunt Louise, Diane, Johnnie Mae, Jo Ann, Birtha, Lynn, and Rita. I love y'all...

My uncles:

My favorite, Uncle Larry, you're such an inspiration... I watched your testimony blossom before my own eyes. God is able... Uncle Henry, Larry, and Ocie, love y'all

To my friends:

Thanks for supporting me through the years... love y'all so much... (Stamps, Paige, Reese, Steward's, Williams, Plaines)

TT, Marilyn...Thanks for keeping the promise to my mother, you've done nothing less.... I'm blessed to have you in my life... I'm forever grateful... Iesha, Tony, Gino love y'all to life....

Linda Reese (Ma)...Thanks for making me the man I am today... I learned so much from you...

Pops (Cedric)...Love you... Thanks for believing in the dream, the vision when it felt like no one else did... Together we gone build an empire...

Mama P...Thank for being there for me. Your spirit is so sound and true.... You took me in as if I was your own... Your prayers, your discernment... Is so on point... I couldn't do it without you...

Billy...Hey, bro not sure where to start... You are my friend, cousin, and my right hand... We have our own book to write... Nothing like having real friends ... Let's get it.... Get rich, and live that good life!

Obie and Tony…My brother's…Love y'all bro... My twenty-year ninjas.

My brother from another mother LB, Craig: Thanks for holding me down.

Kim…You still one of my favorite cuzins…

John (security), Red, Young Buck, Dustin, JoJo, K-Ci, and Tiny… Love yall... Ginuwine, thanks for being a stand up guy, and true friend. Joe Love, Willie Neal, J Neal, Gage…love you. Y'all some of my favorite ninjas. Bobbie…I love you. Thanks for the good times…always family. Thanks for standing in the trenches with me.

Kevyn Black…Thanks for coming to our studio in Chicago (5550 Bloomingdale) on that cold winter day, 1994...hearing what Shorty had to offer, and going back to Interscope and Death Row records, and creating the buzz for us...(Crucial conflict, Fuskeee, and myself)

DJ Quik, the true living legend…Thanks for being my big brother, and taking me in when I moved to LA.. What better way to enter the music business, and record my first major records? David Blake.... The councilor, the holistic doctor, the technical genius... Salute big bro! Thanks for helping me mold a sound...

To my baby…Beatbyburnie…I love you, thanks for loving me back...I believe in you…can't wait to see you grow and prosper in your gift... Your are the master of beat… I love you. Let's grow together…

Rip Anthony. I miss you so much...I appreciate the strength you gave me. I cherish the time we spent together. Your passing hurt me to the core, but gave me life.... I will forever say your name and keep your legacy alive...

In dedication to you #loveagainstsuicideandhate

My Chicago, Detroit, Mississippi, PA, and Cali family... Thanks for holding me down... Trumbull, Chicago Ave, North Ave, Drake Street family, love y'all...

Companies: Willie Watkins (Douglasville) thanks Greg, Mary's BBQ, J's Signature, Beatbyburnie, ESMG, Lewis Agency. Thank you.

My team: Billy, Tracey, Kimberla, Cedric (Pops), Mama P, Tomorrow, Tommy (Red), Wendy, Dustin, Beatbyburnie.

Shanon.... Thanks for helping me kick this back off, and for getting me focused on getting this story done. Thanks for your long nights.... I owe u true Chitown love...

Tara the Editor... Thanks for helping me bring my story to life... Thanks for being so professional; I look forward to working on many other projects with you love. You...hurry up to the A.

To my haters, naysayers, and people casting me to hell and all that other shit. I'm not moved, because I know when it comes to Jesus, nothing can separate me from his blood. Besides, your hate can't defeat the love that I have inside of me and the love that God has for me!! Your thoughts will no longer affect me as they once had.

To my fans, supporters, Facebook family, Instagrammers, and all...thank you for staying behind me, and following me throughout my career. I hope you continue to follow me on my journey. You are welcome to take this ride along with me, as we travel to another place!!

I guess I've shared everything but a song, close your eyes as I sing a song inside of your heart....

Please visit www.iamdannyboy.com for updates.

Printed in Great Britain
by Amazon